This book belongs to:

_____

_____

BLUEBELL
Practice Makes Perfect
Handwriting Workbook

1st Edition

Neena Bluebell

BLUEBELL Practice Makes Perfect Handwriting Workbook
by Neena Bluebell

ISBN-13: 978-1725999138
ISBN-10: 1725999137

PREFACE

A Note to Teachers and Parents

andwriting is a valuable skill. The Practice Makes Perfect Handwriting Workbook aims to help little children learn handwriting in a fun and easy way.

The book begins with a pre-writing skills section that introduces children to the fundamental strokes needed to build a foundation for clear handwriting. The next two sections provide step-by-step instructions for writing uppercase and lowercase letters. My book provides ample practice for tracing as well as writing the letters independently. It aims to reinforce learning with an alphabet coloring page section including lots of pictures to color and words to trace.

I hope that the children enjoy learning from this book as much as I have enjoyed creating it!

Best Wishes,

Neena

TABLE OF CONTENTS

Section 1: Pre-Writing Skills - Trace and Learn   1

Vertical Lines 2
Horizontal Lines 3
Slanted Lines 4
Trace the Patterns 6
Plus (+) Shapes.. 12
Cross (X) Shapes 13
Curves 14
Circles, Clockwise 16
Circles, Counterclockwise... 17
Arcs, Clockwise... 18
Arcs, Counterclockwise... 19
Trace the Patterns.. 20
Trace and Color the Shapes! 23

Section 2: Trace and Write   25

A a 26
B b 28
C c 30
D d 32
E e 34
F f 36
G g 38
H h 40
I i 42
J j 44
K k 46
L l 48
M m 50

Section 2 cont. on next page

Section 2: Trace and Write (cont.)

N n 52

O o 54

P p 56

Q q 58

R r 60

S s 62

T t 64

U u 66

V v 68

W w 70

X x 72

Y y 74

Z z 76

Section 3: Review and Practice   79

Review the steps for writing uppercase letters 80

Practice writing uppercase letters 81

Review the steps for writing lowercase letters 82

Practice writing lowercase letters 83

More practice worksheets 84

Section 4:   Alphabet Coloring Pages

A a 98
B b 99
C c 100
D d 101
E e 102
F f 103
G g 104
H h 105
I i 106
J j 107
K k 108
L l 109
M m 110
N n 111
O o 112
P p 113
Q q 114
R r 115
S s 116
T t 117
U u 118
V v 119
W w 120
X x 121
Y y 122
Z z 123

Section
1

Pre-Writing Skills

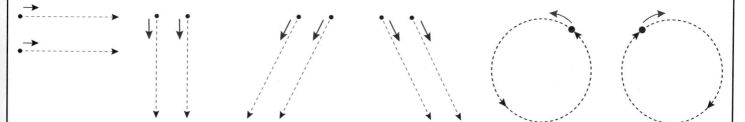

Trace

and

Learn

Vertical Lines
Trace From Top to Bottom

Horizontal Lines
Trace From Left to Right

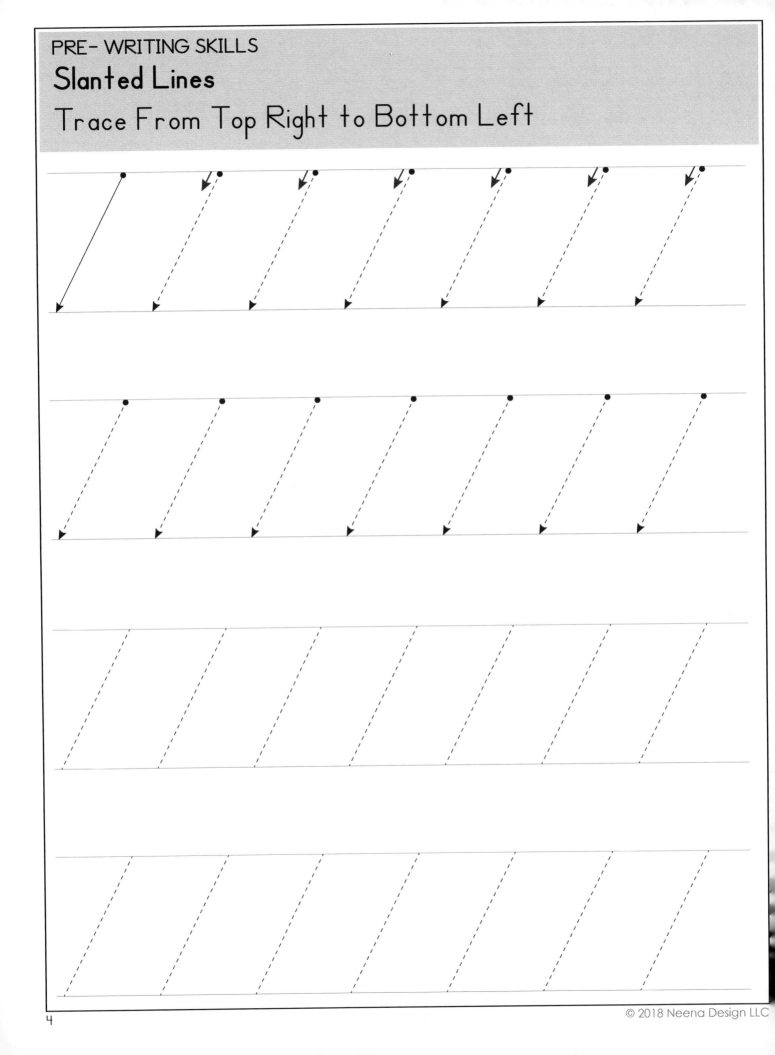

Slanted Lines

Trace From Top Left to Bottom Right

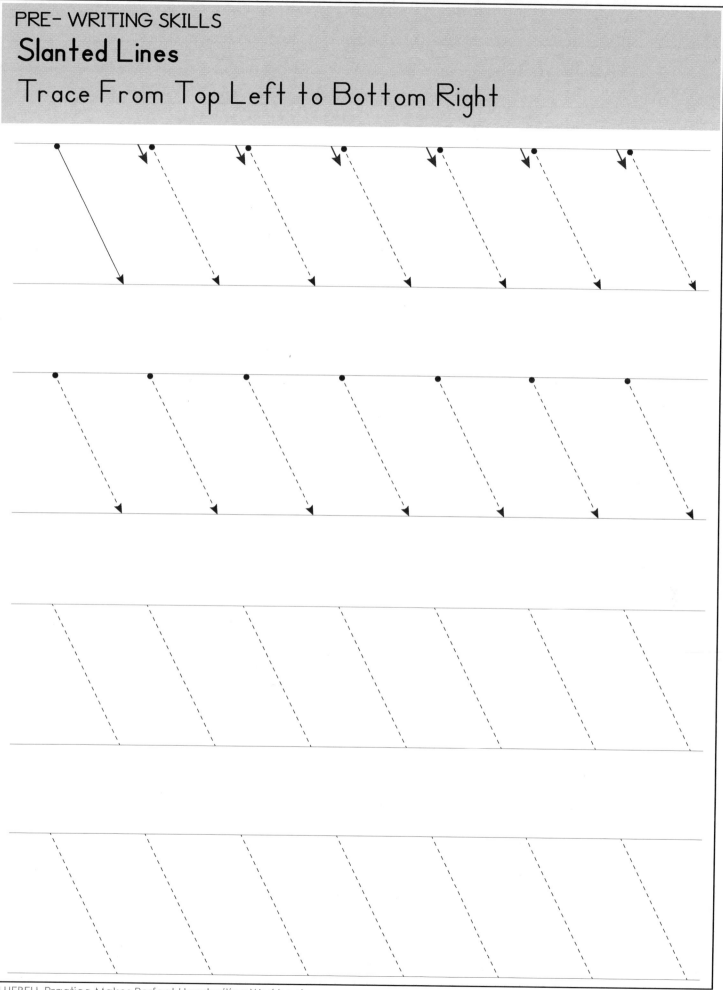

Trace the Patterns

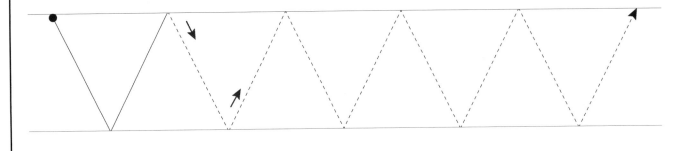

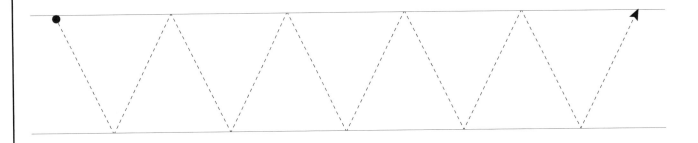

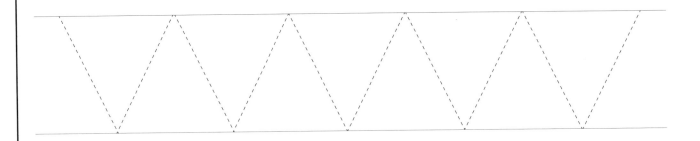

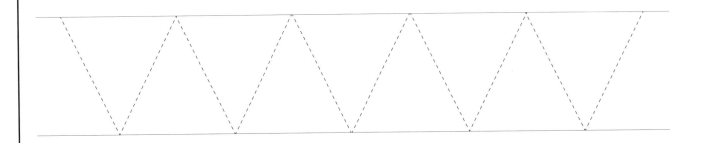

Trace the Patterns

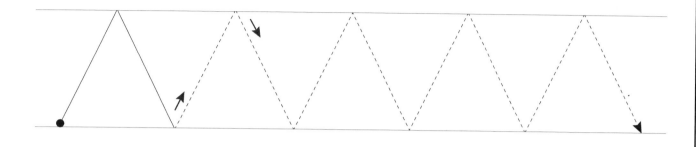

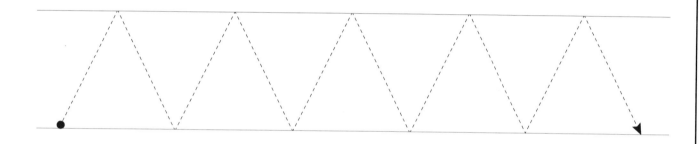

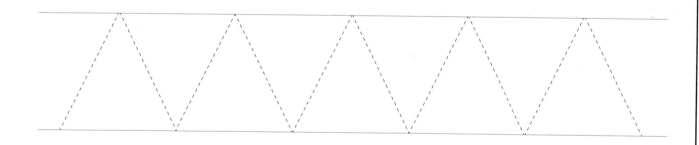

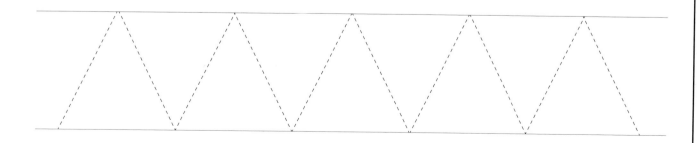

Trace the Patterns

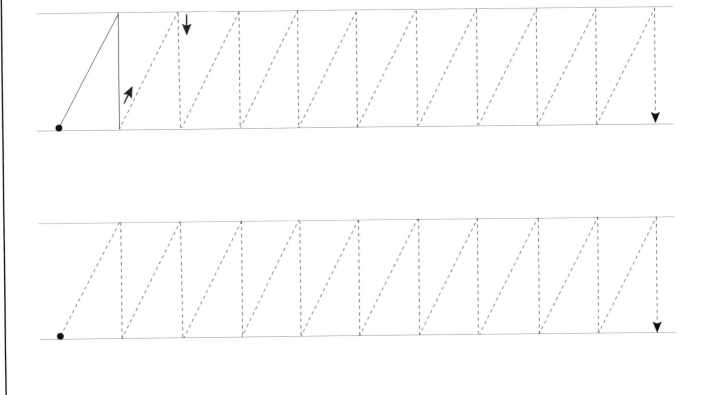

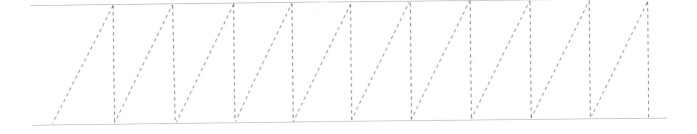

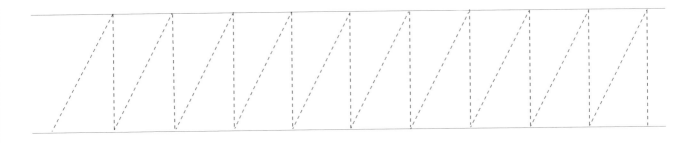

Trace the Patterns

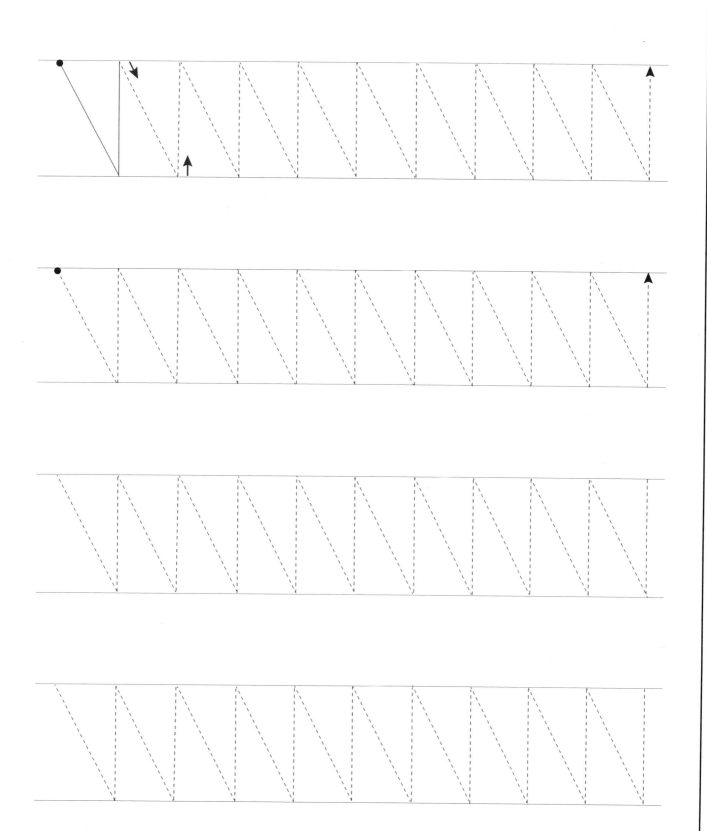

Trace the Patterns

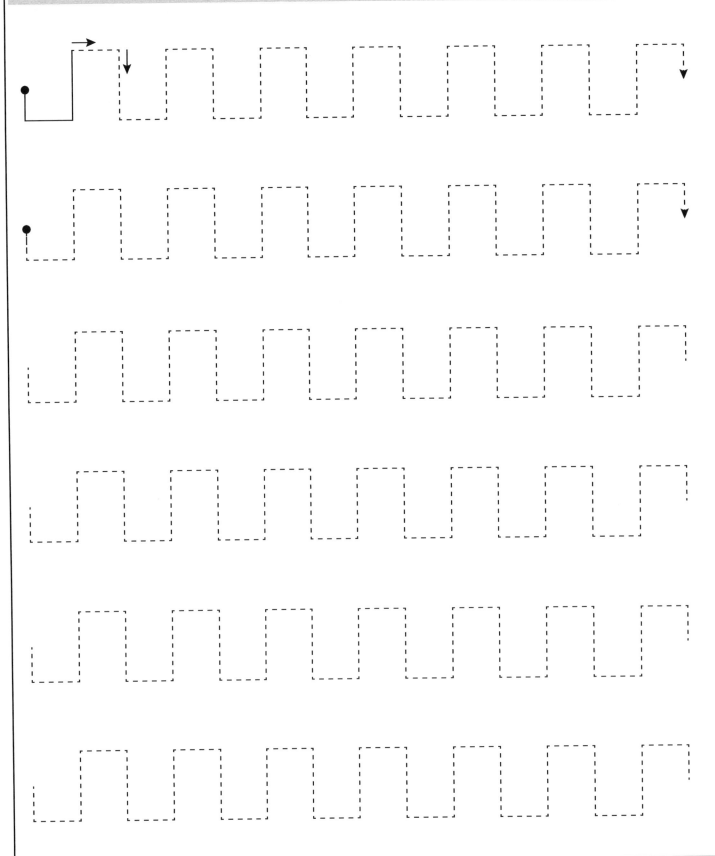

Trace the Patterns

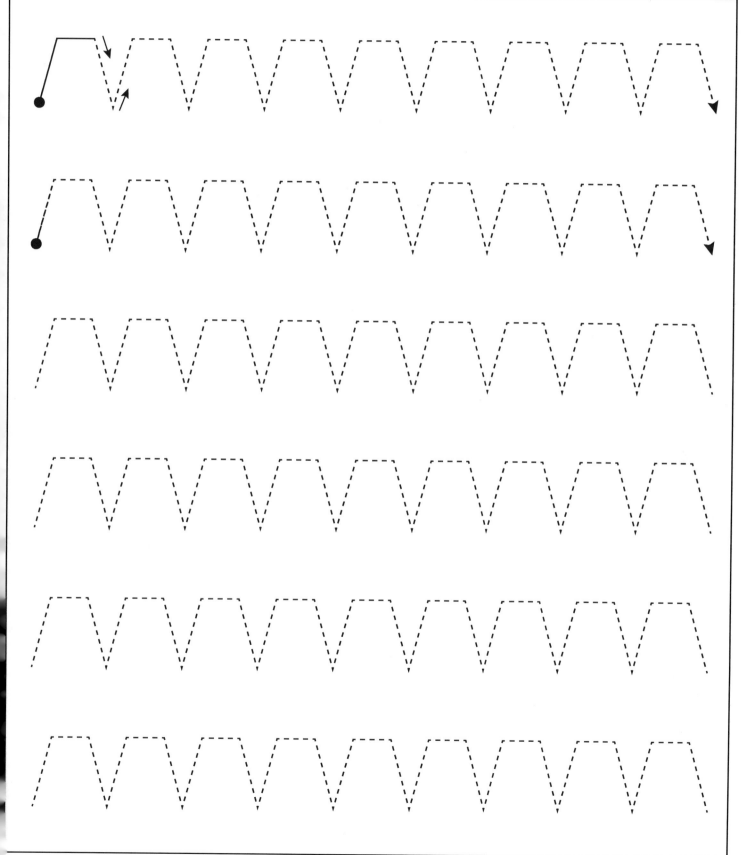

Trace the ✚ Shapes

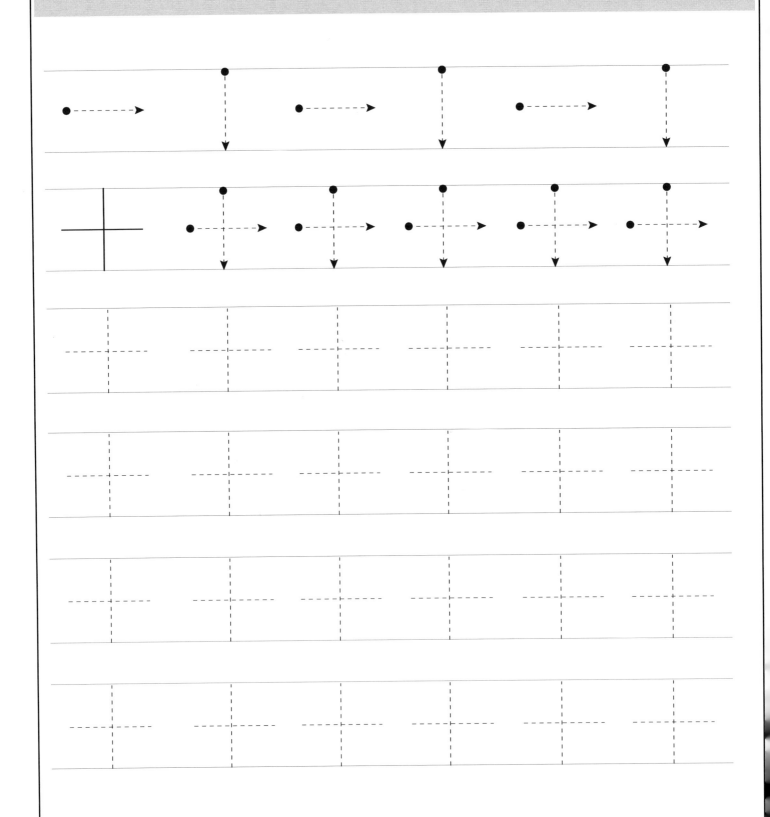

Trace the ✗ Shapes

Trace the Curves

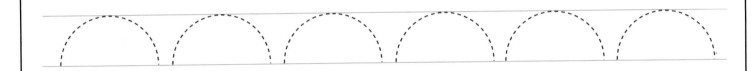

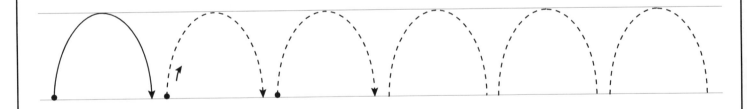

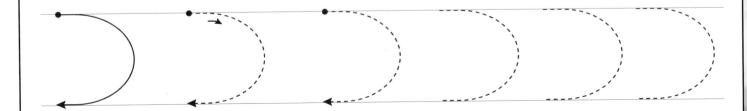

PRE- WRITING SKILLS

Trace the Curves

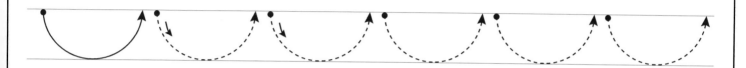

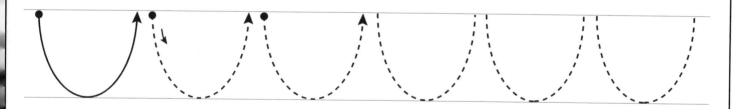

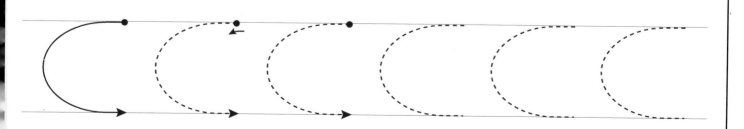

Circles – Trace Clockwise

(FORWARD in the direction of a clock's hands)

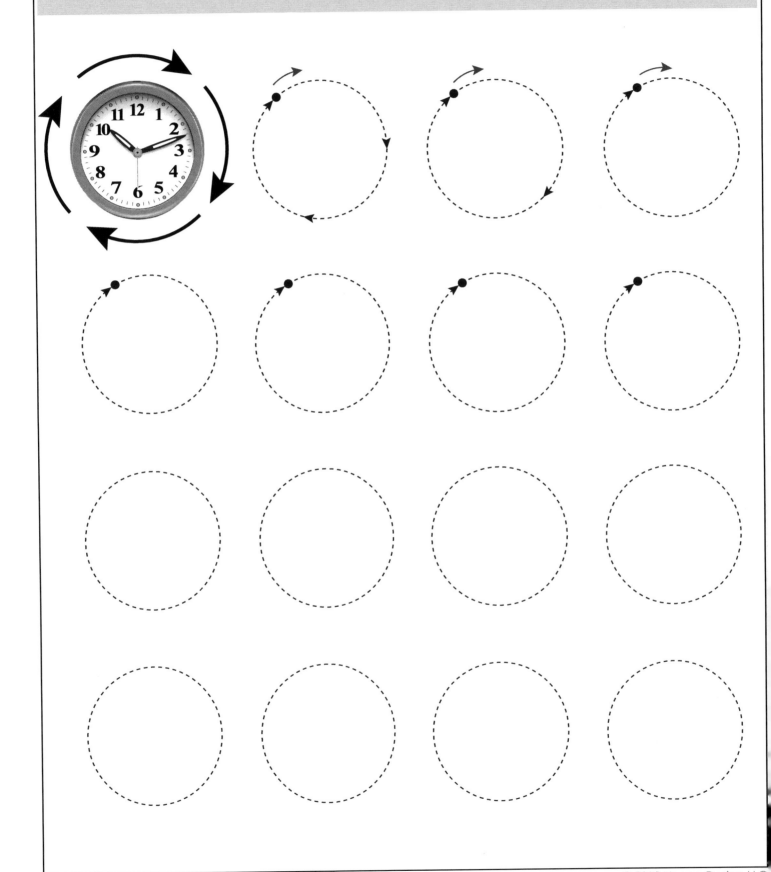

Circles - Trace Counterclockwise

(in the direction OPPOSITE to that of a clock's hands)

Arcs – Trace Counterclockwise

(in the direction OPPOSITE to that of a clock's hands)

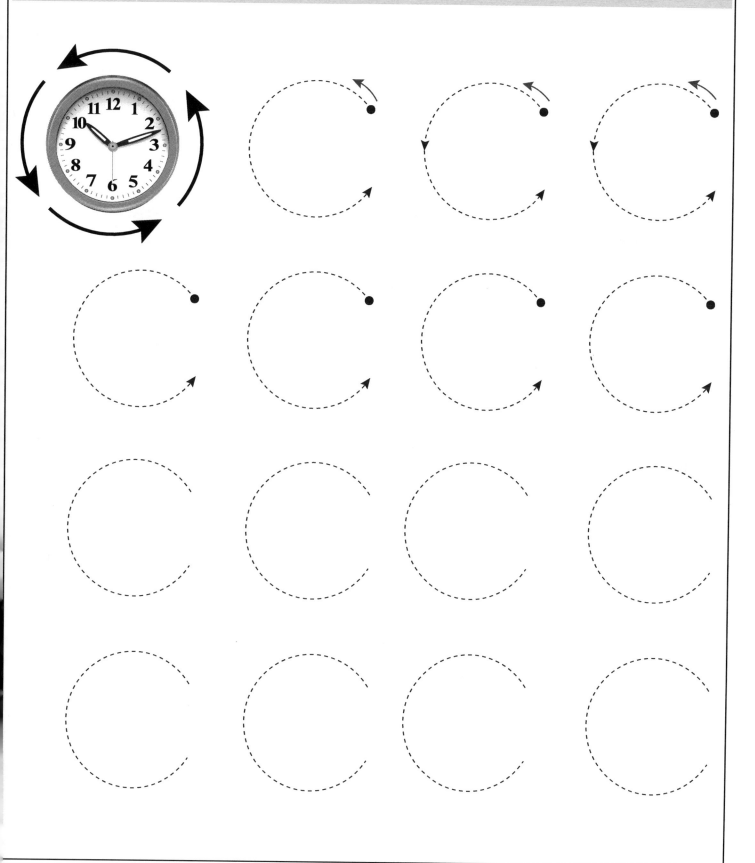

Trace the Patterns

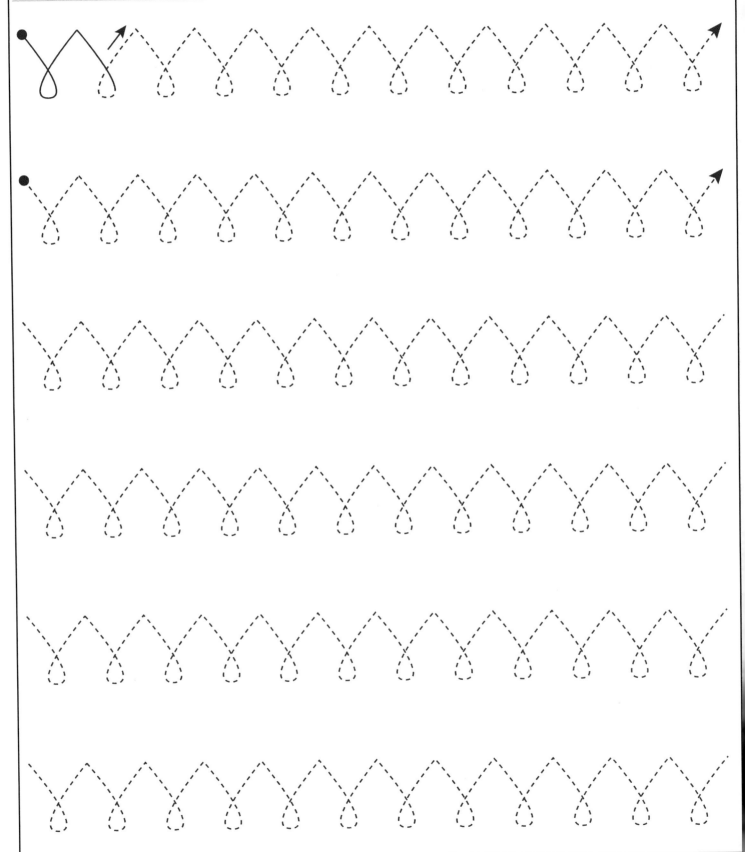

Trace the Patterns

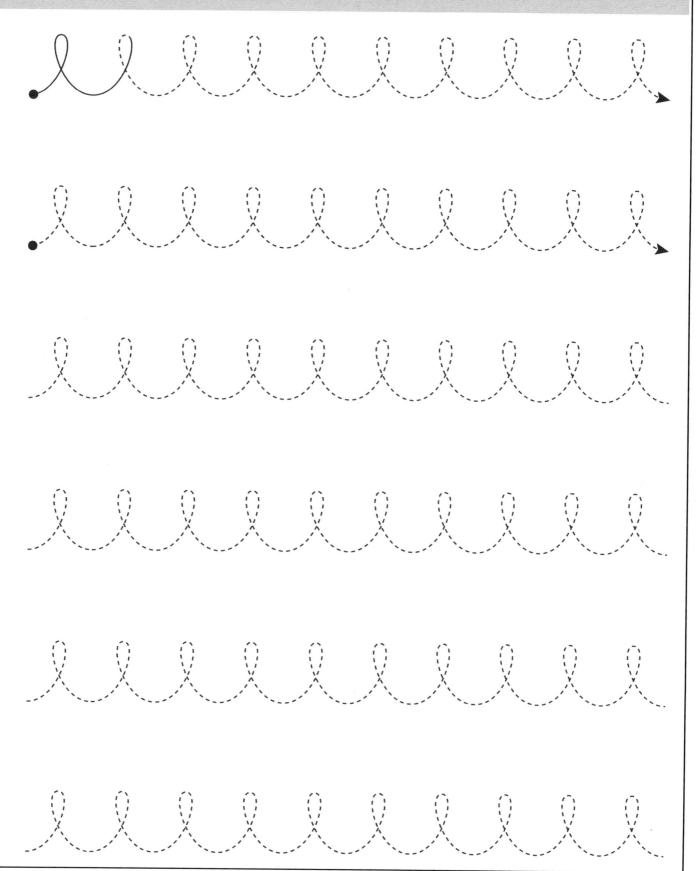

Trace the Patterns

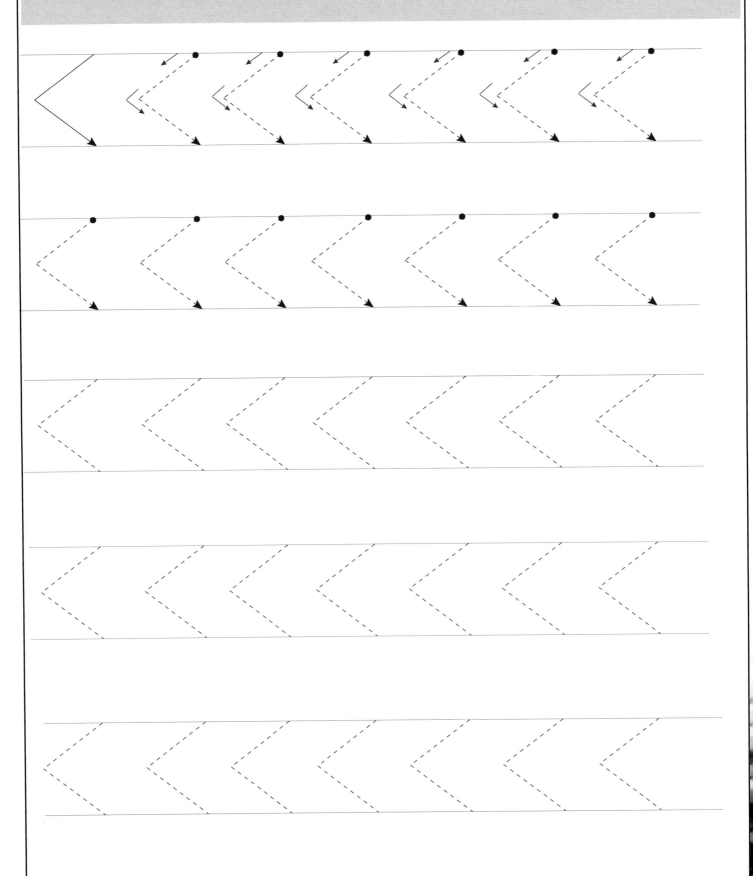

Trace and Color the Shapes!

Section

2

and

Write

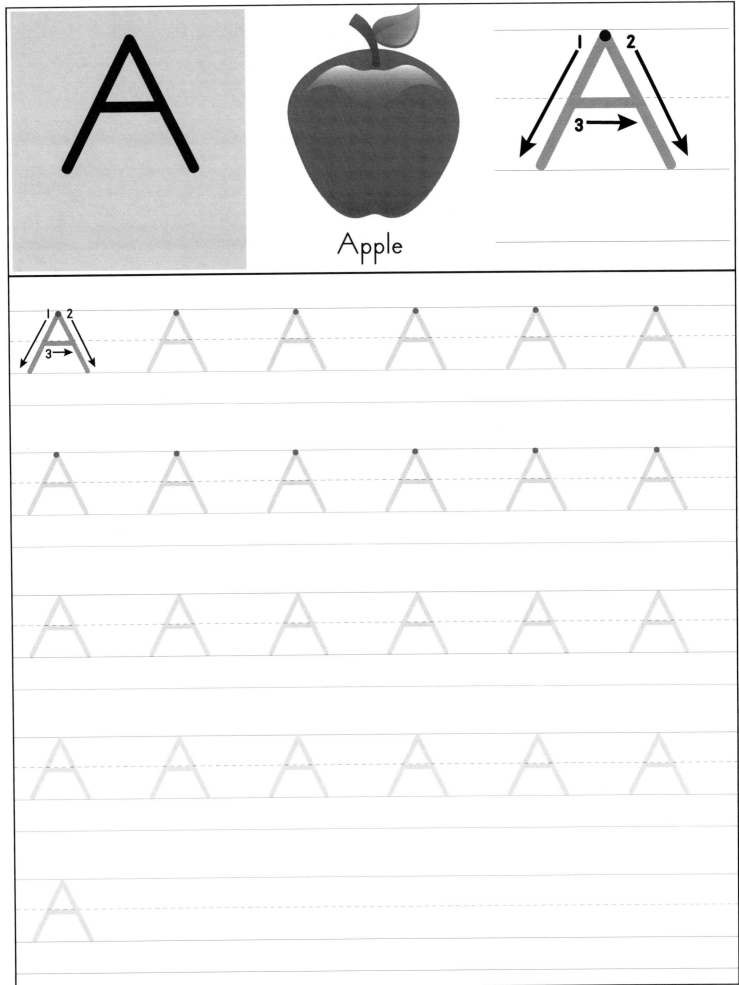

Apple

Ant

B

Butterfly

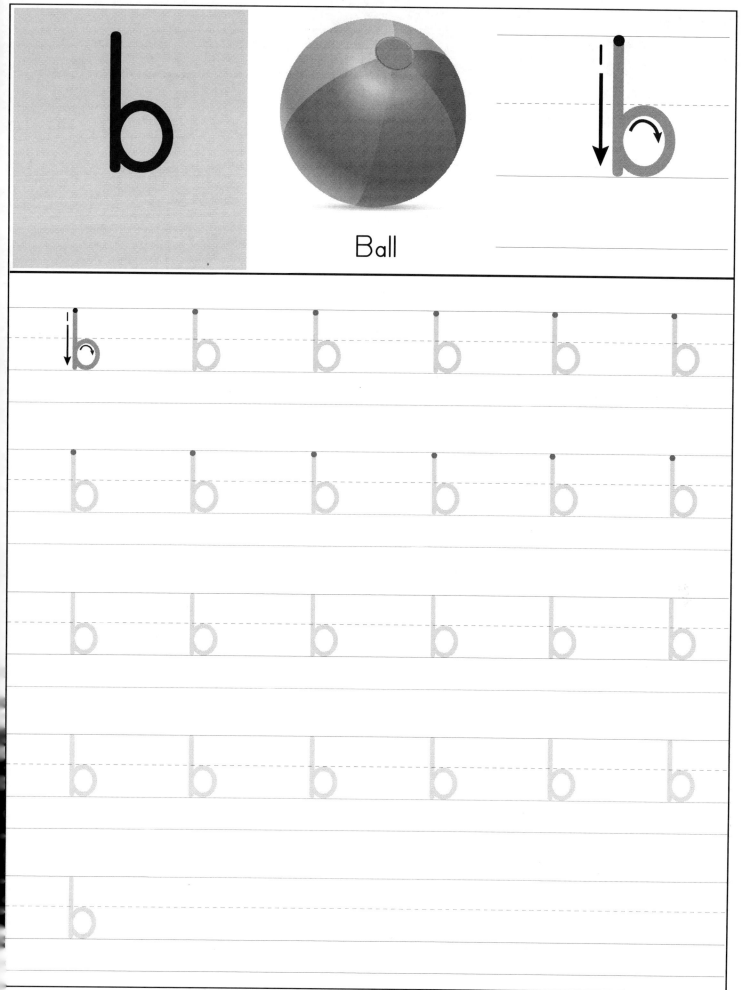

Ball

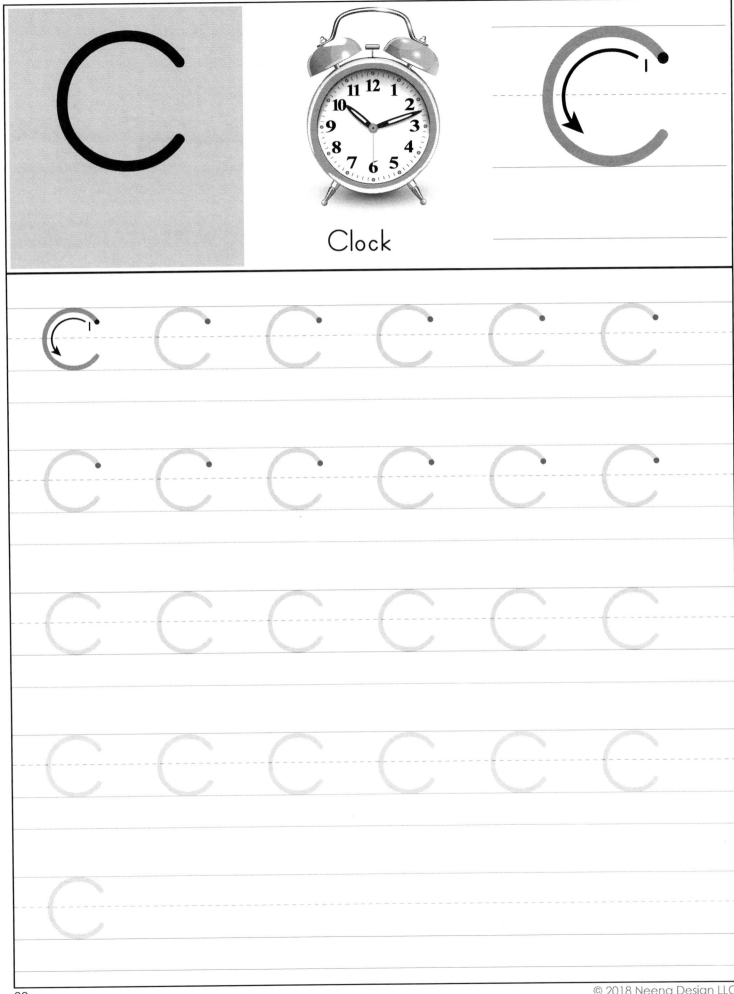

Clock

Carousel

Drum

Dolphin

Elephant

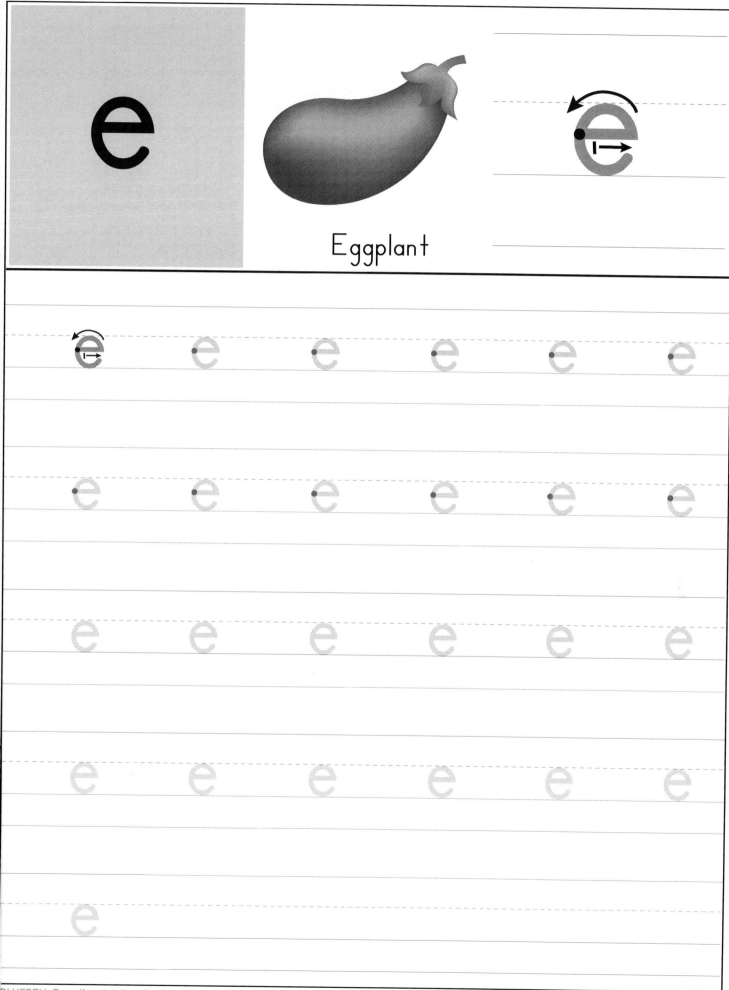

Eggplant

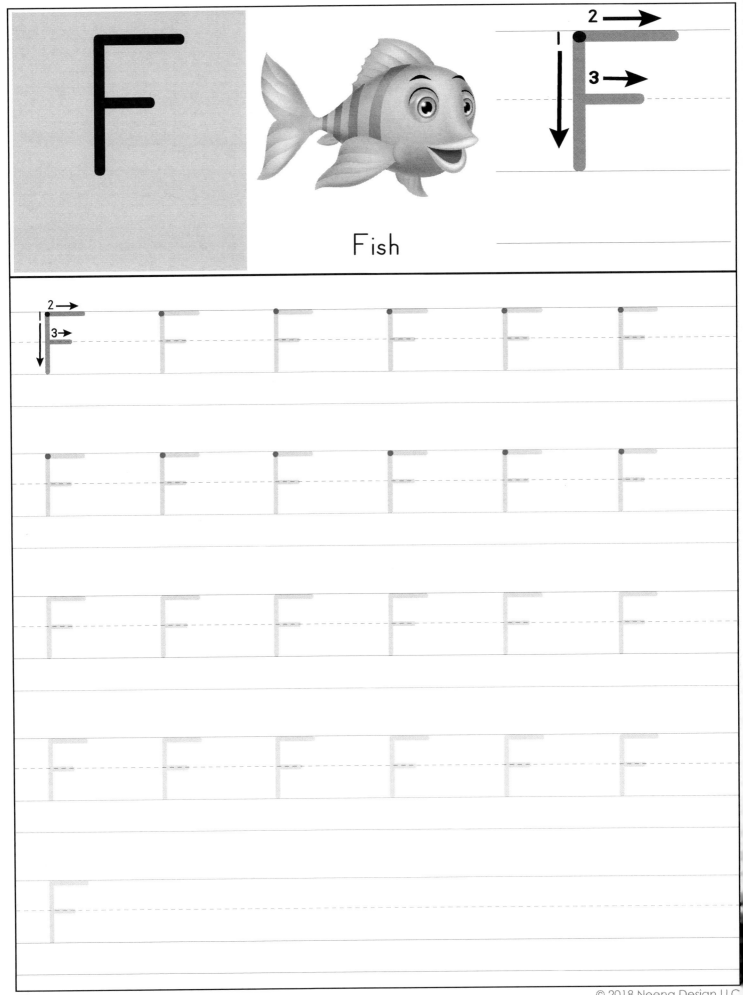

Fish

Fox

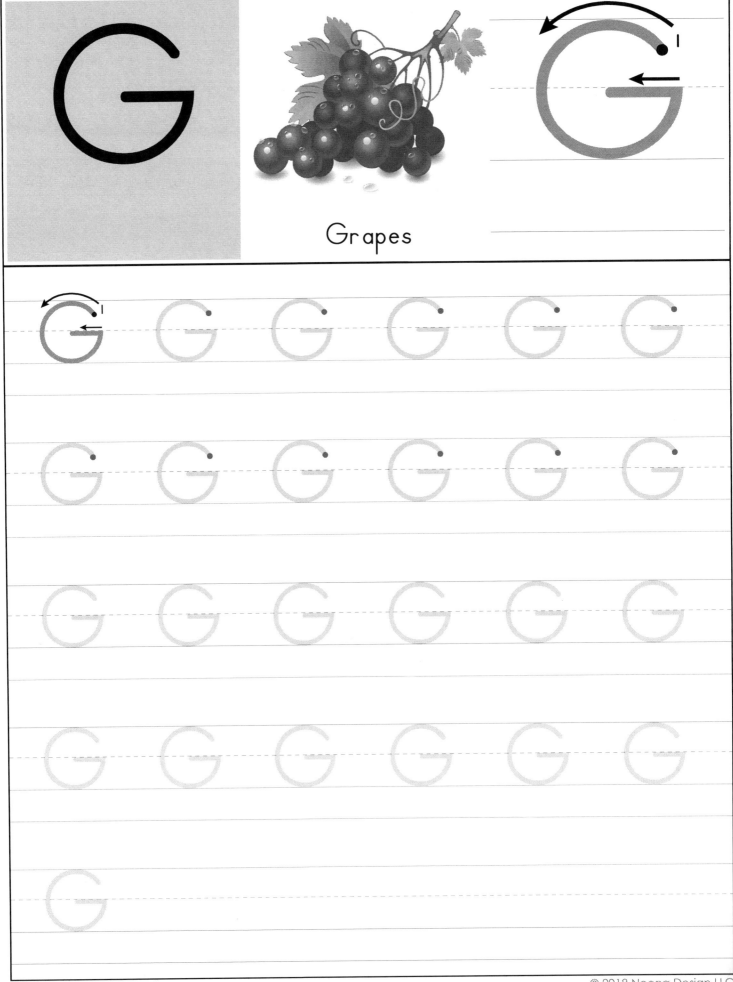

Grapes

g

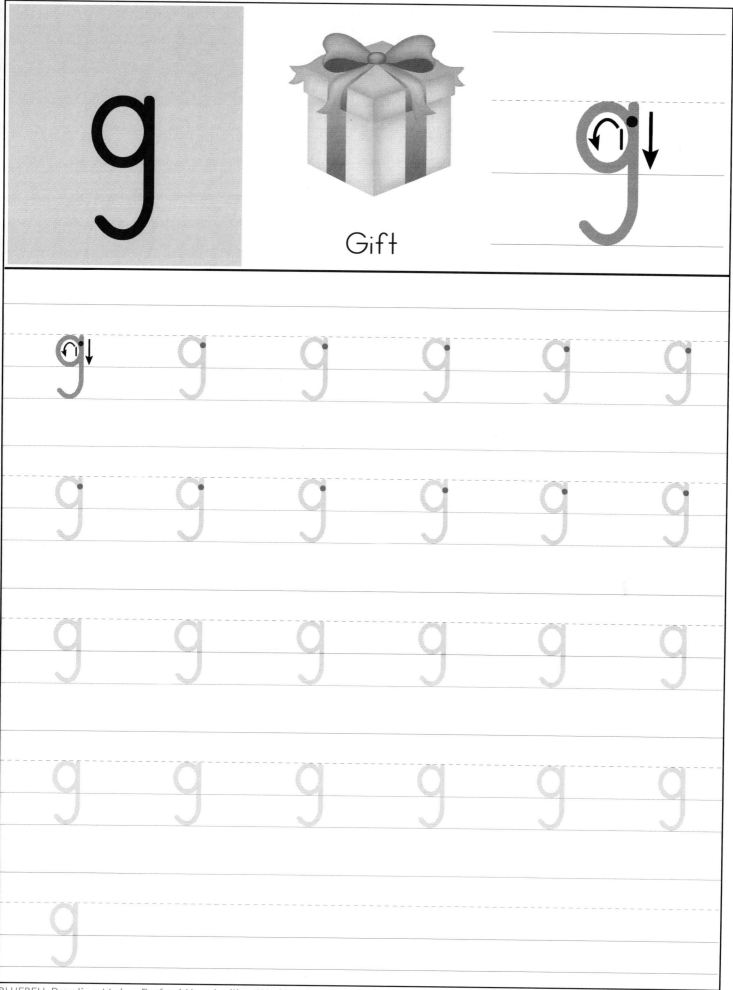

Gift

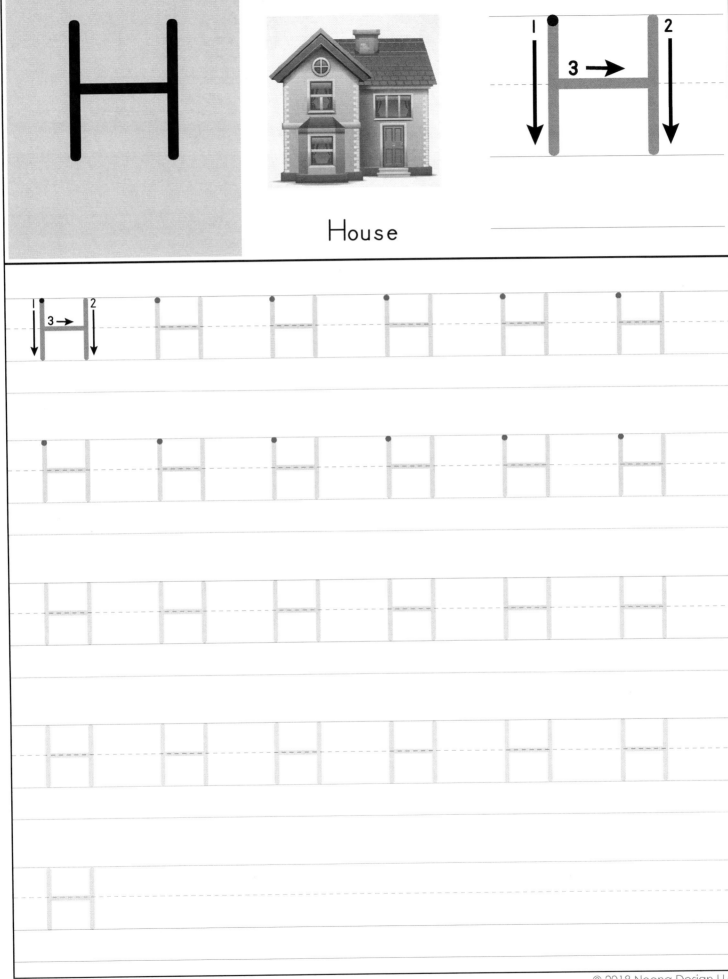

House

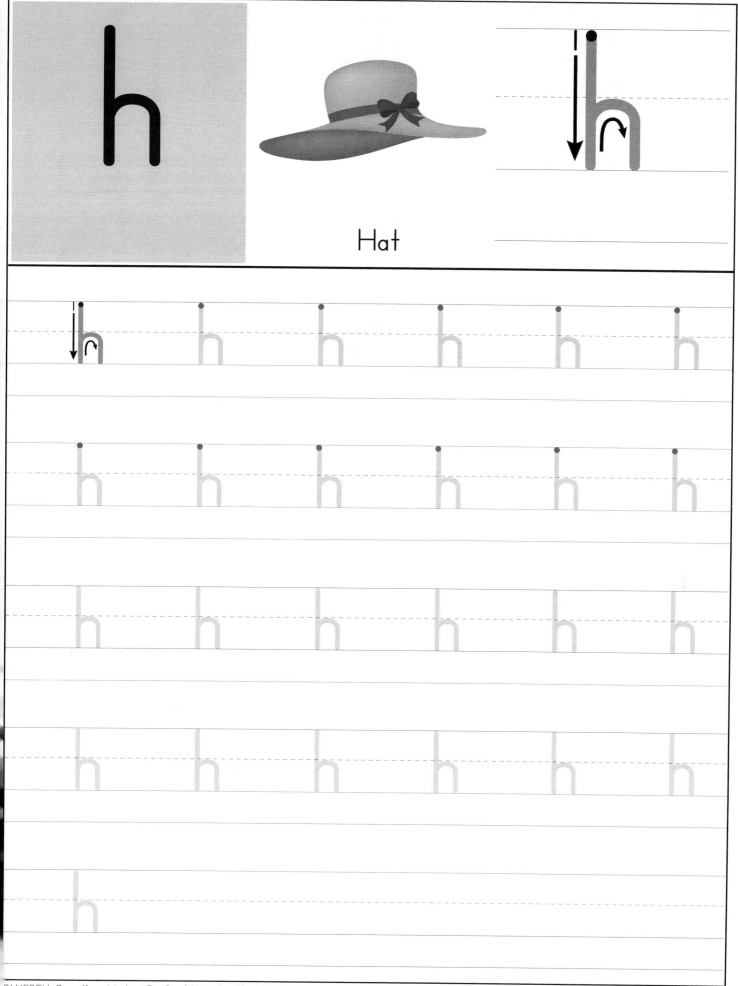

Hat

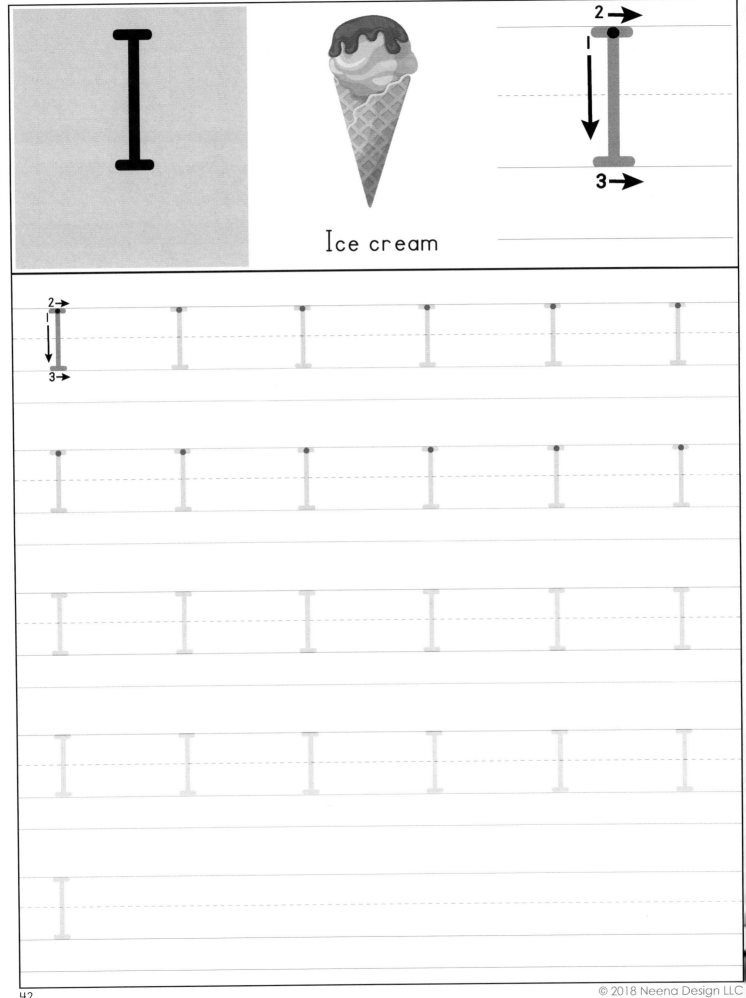

Ice cream

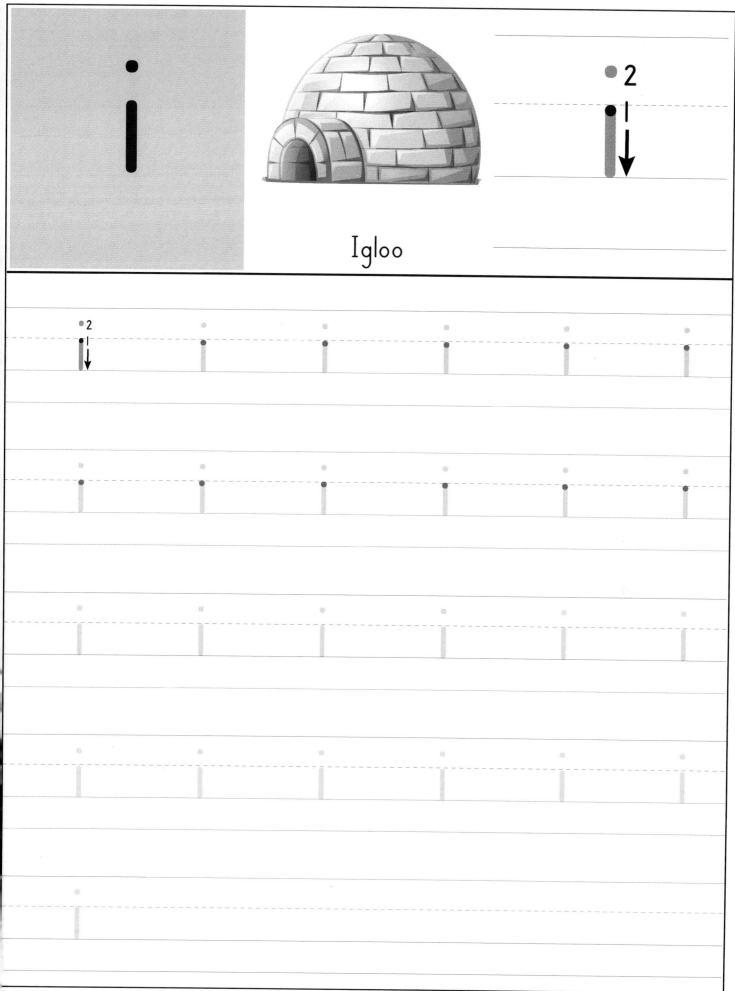

Igloo

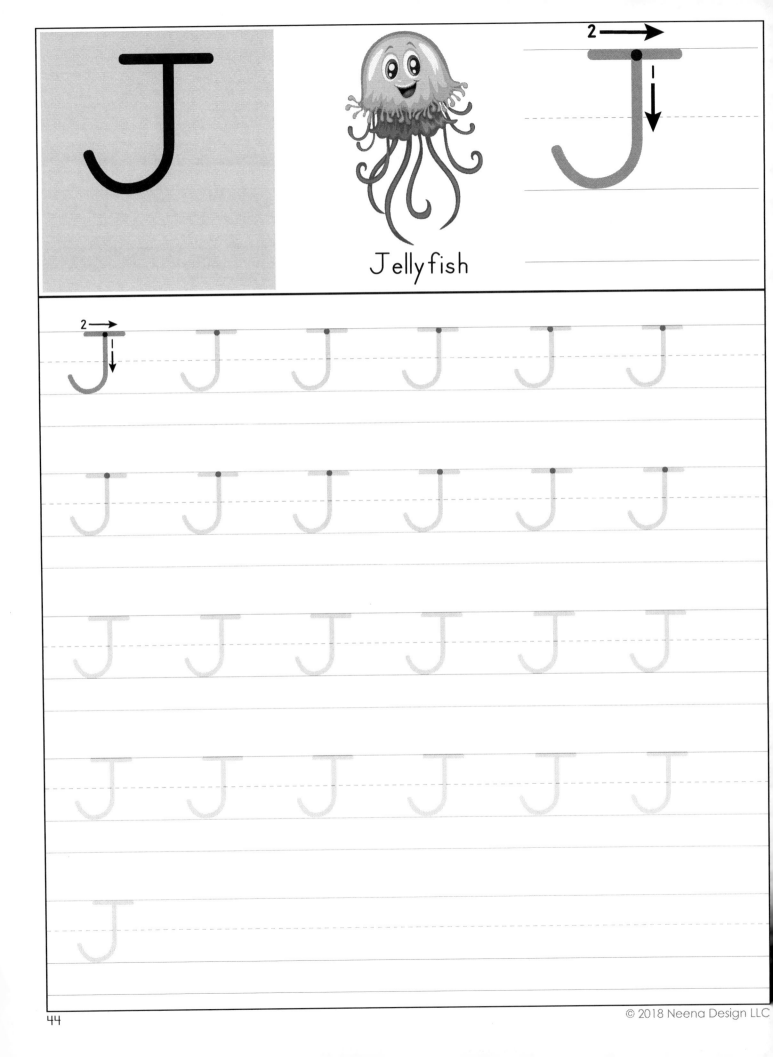

Jellyfish

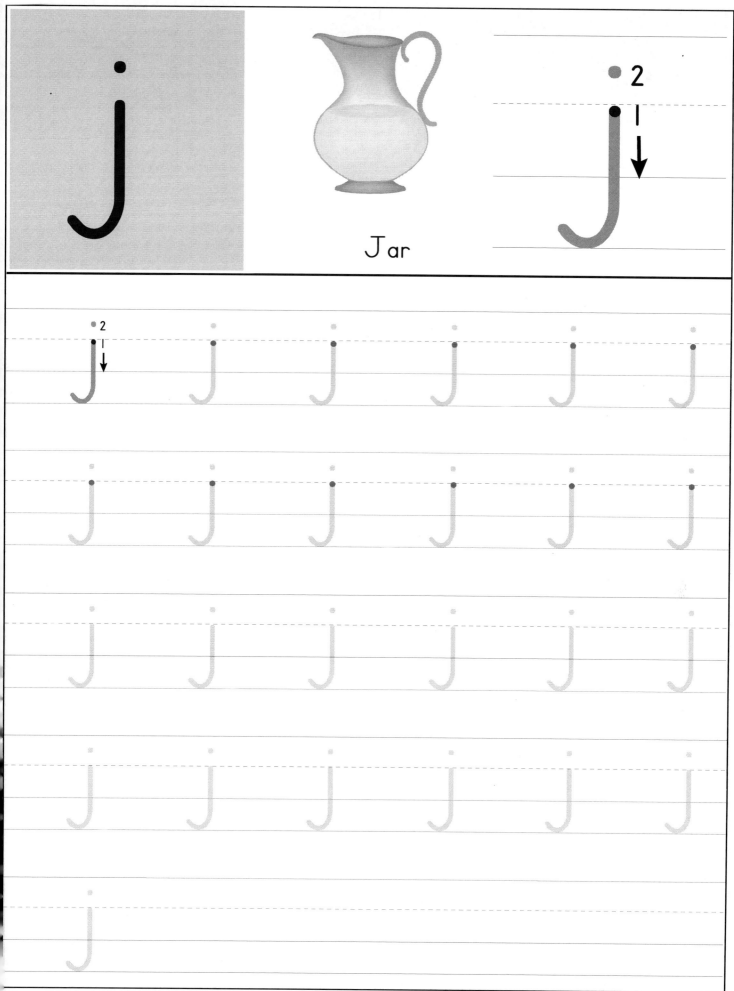

Jar

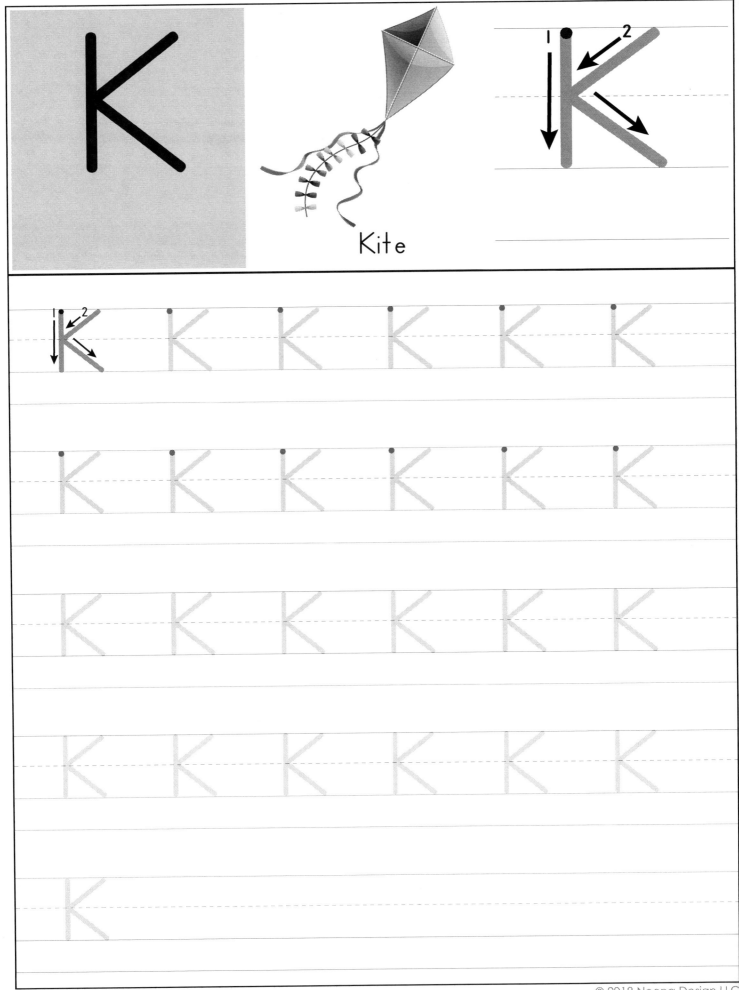

Kite

Kangaroo

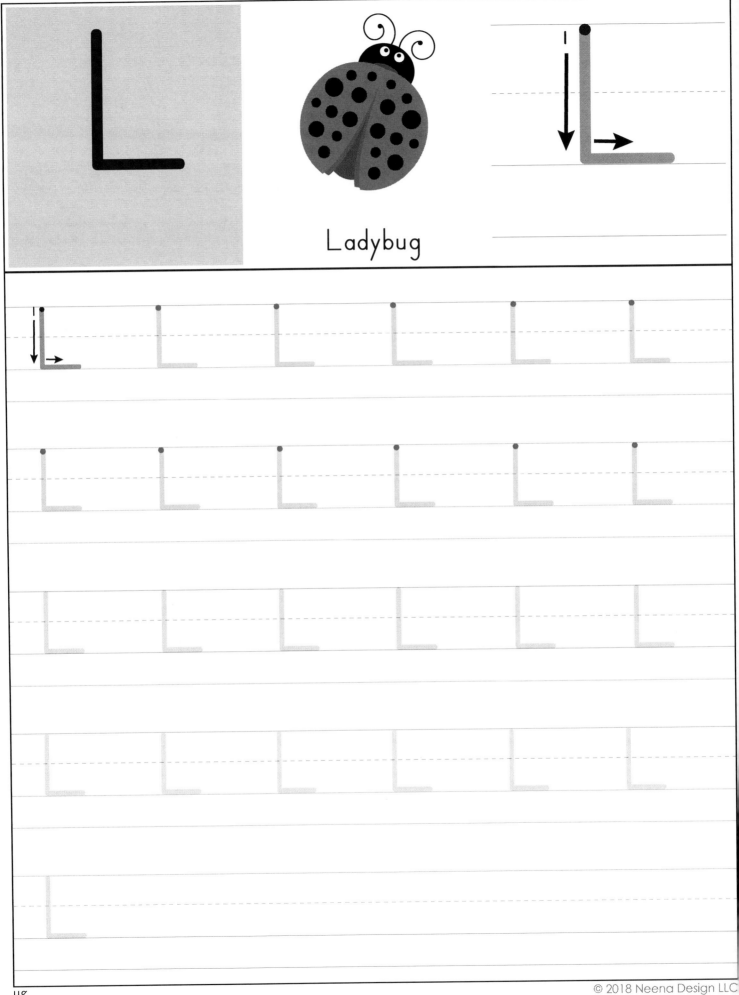

Ladybug

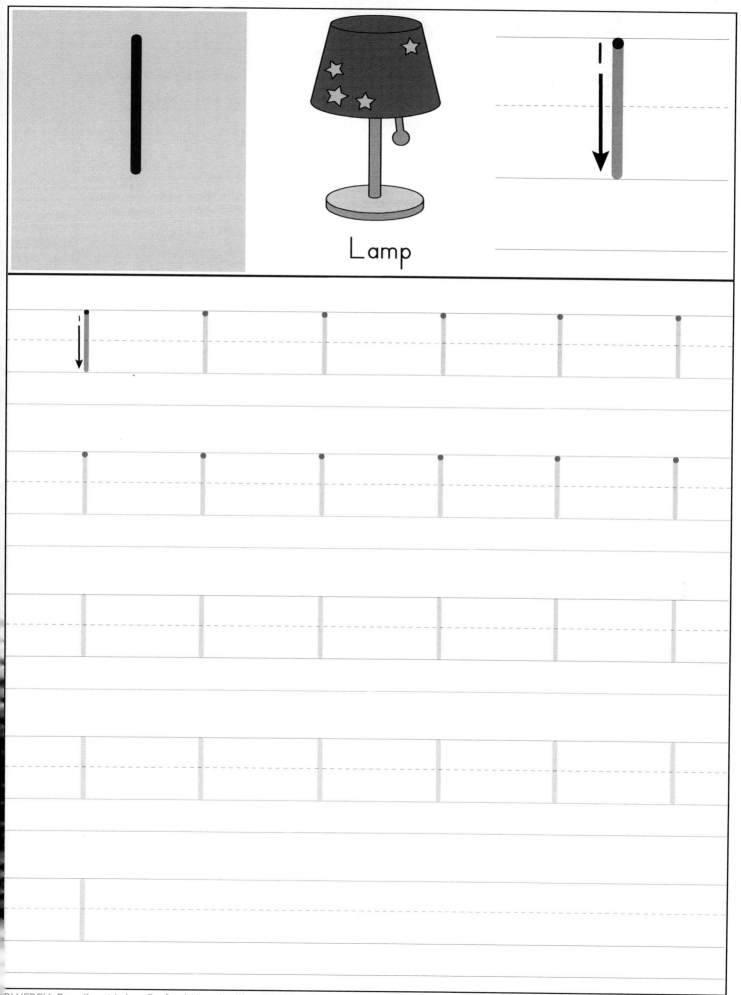

Lamp

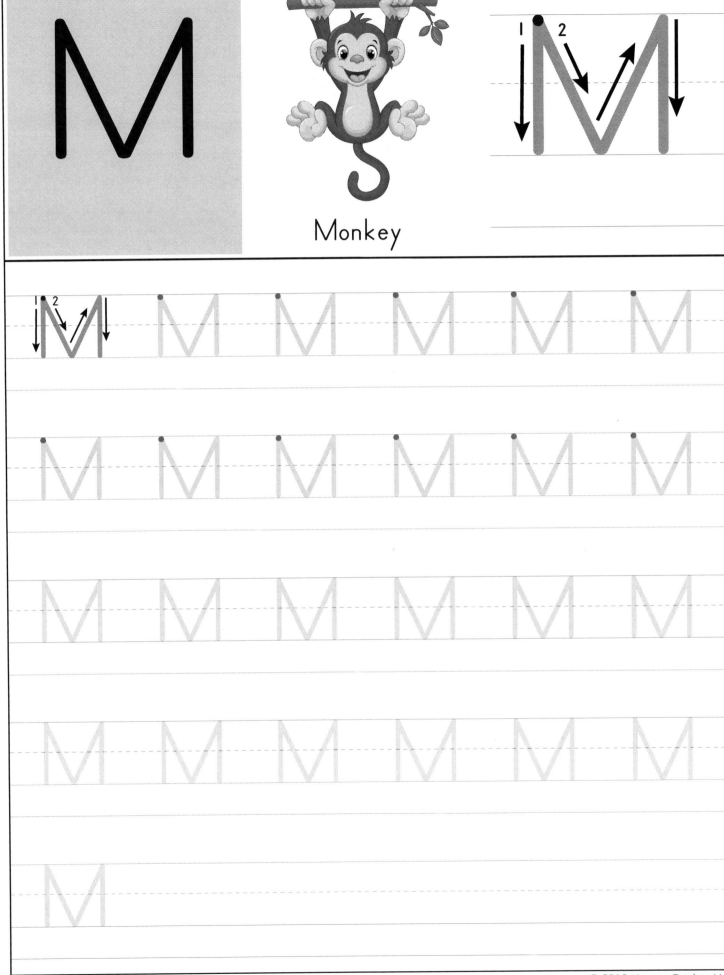

Monkey

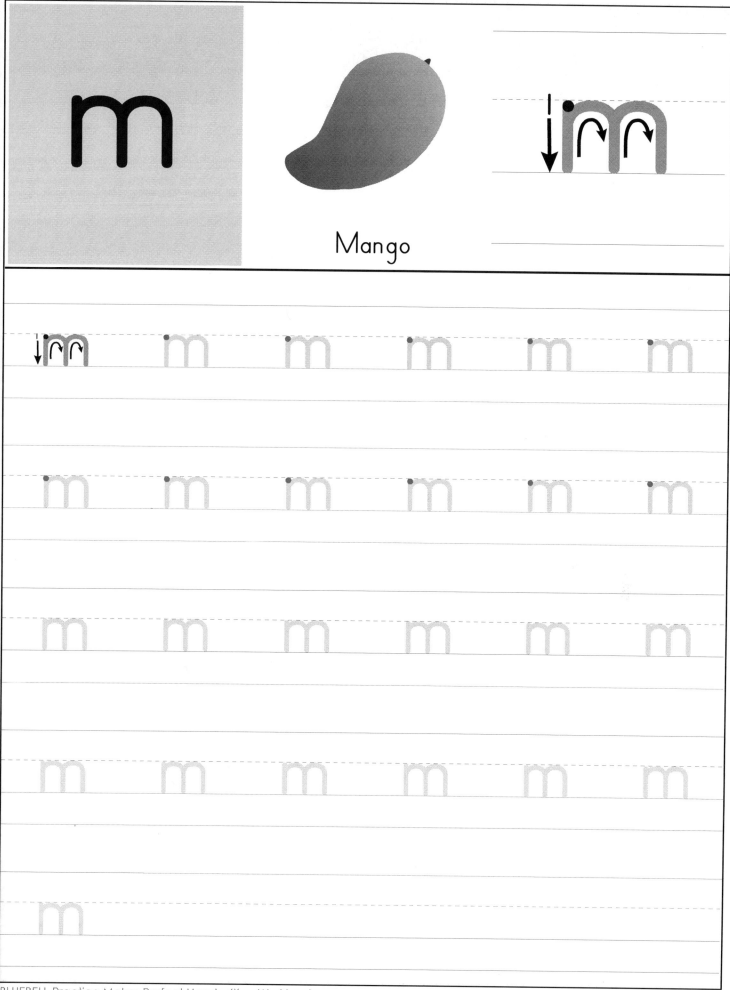

Mango

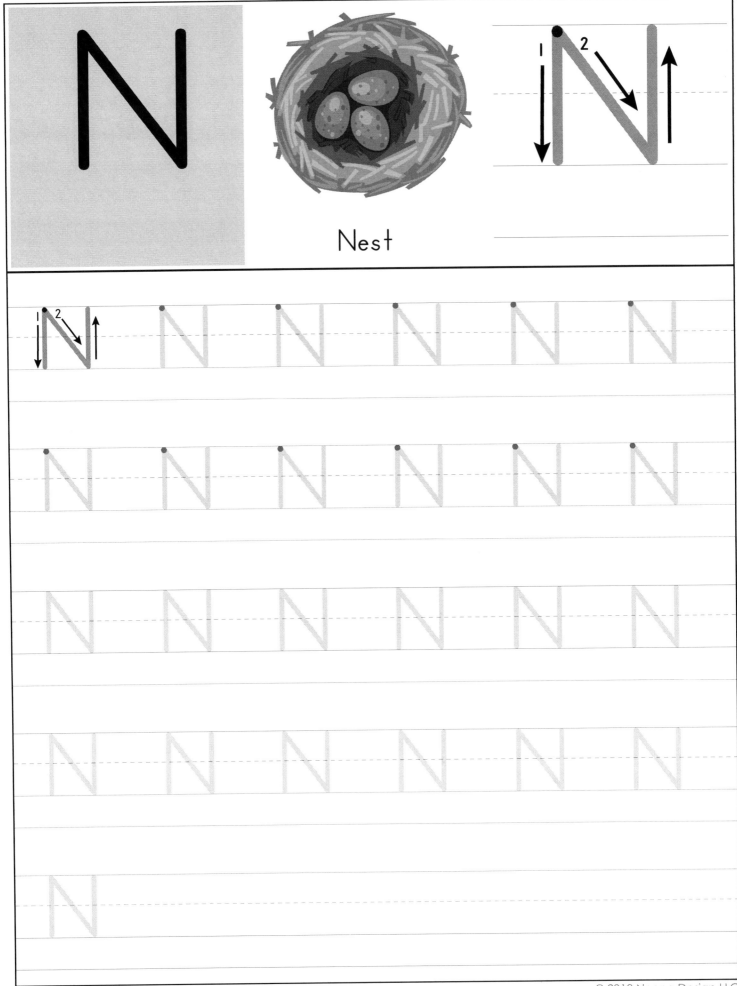

Nest

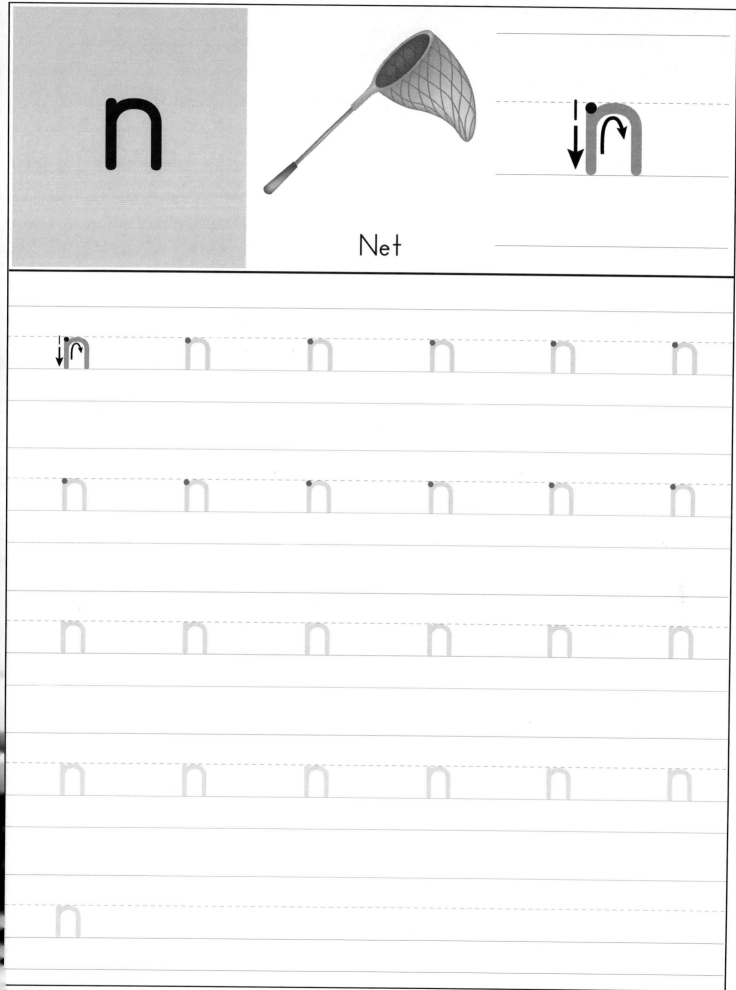

Net

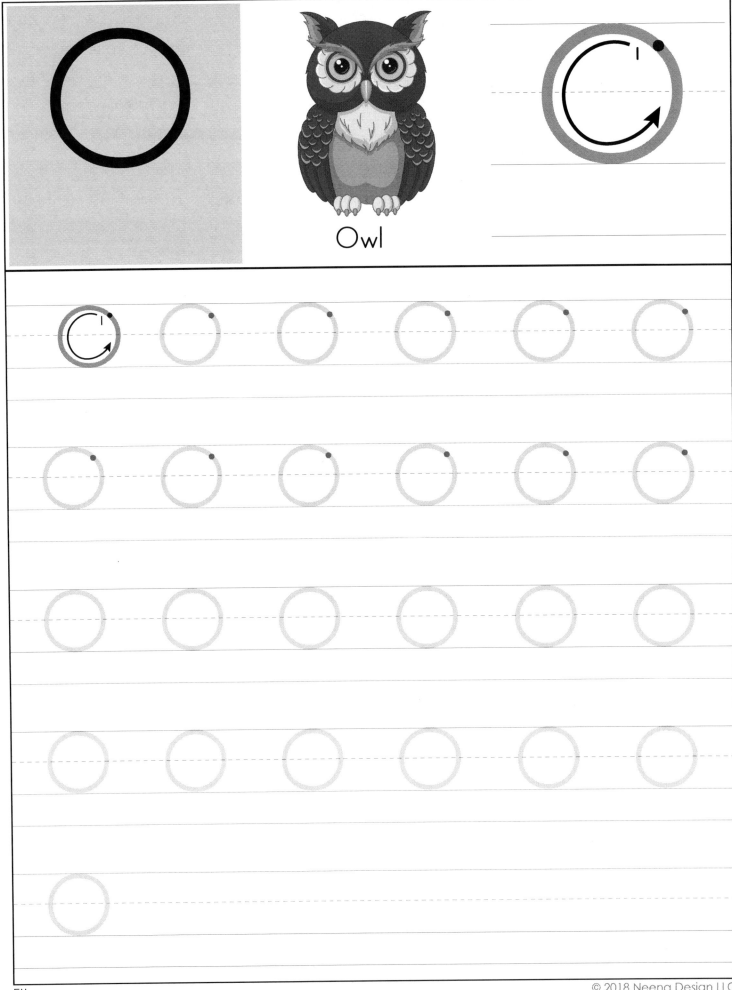

Owl

Onion

P

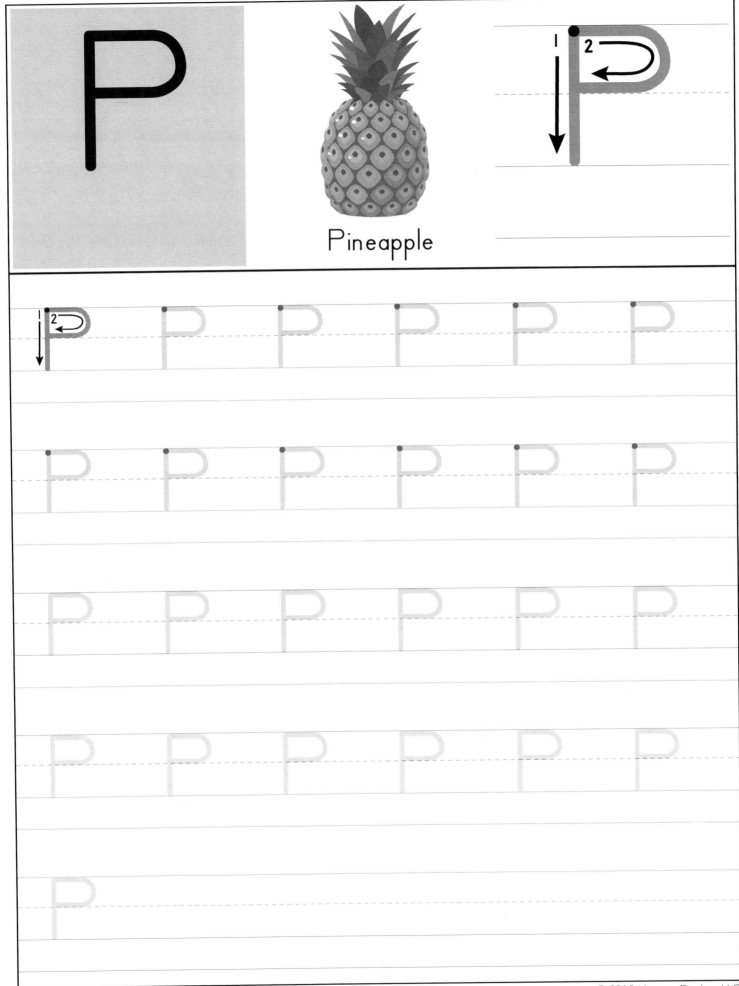

Pineapple

Parrot

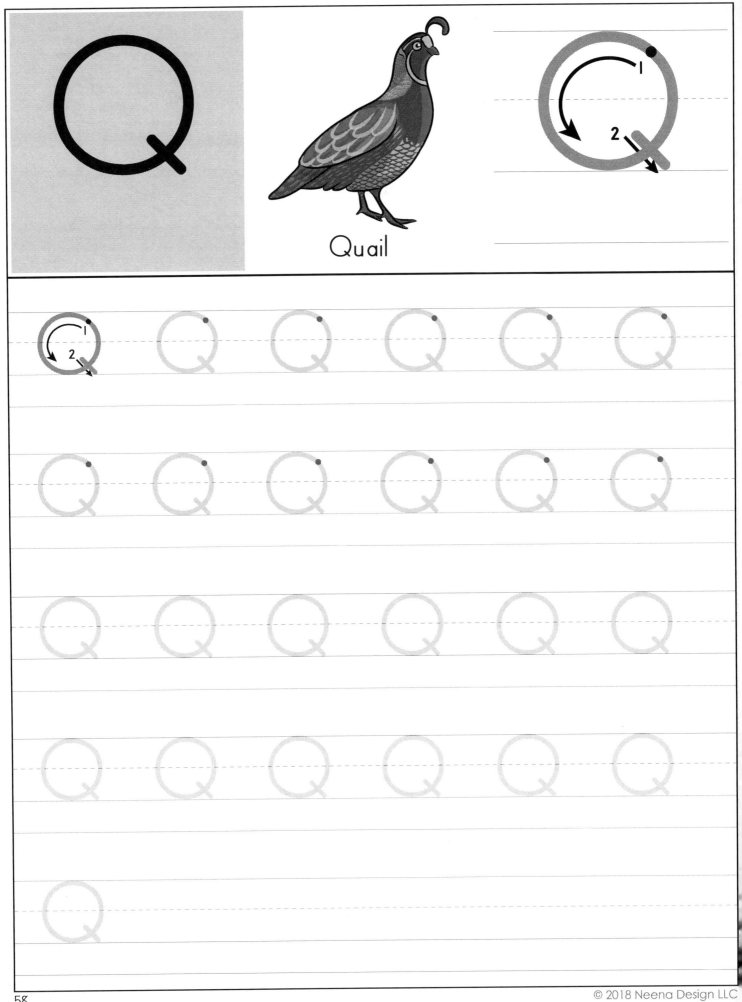

Quail

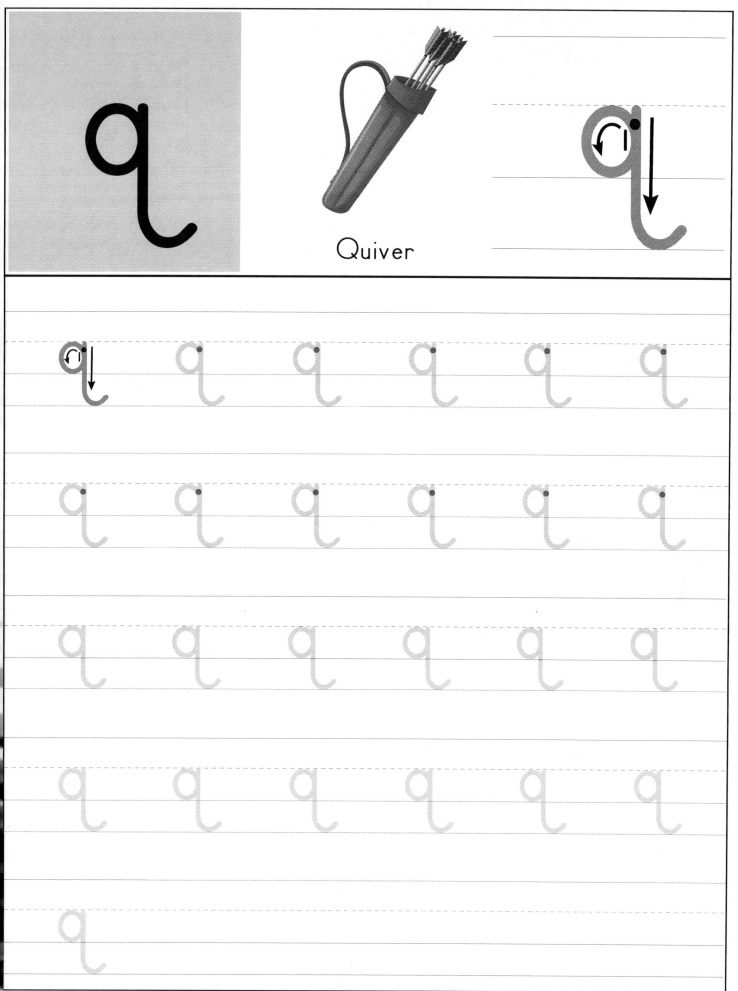

Quiver

R

Rainbow

r

Rabbit

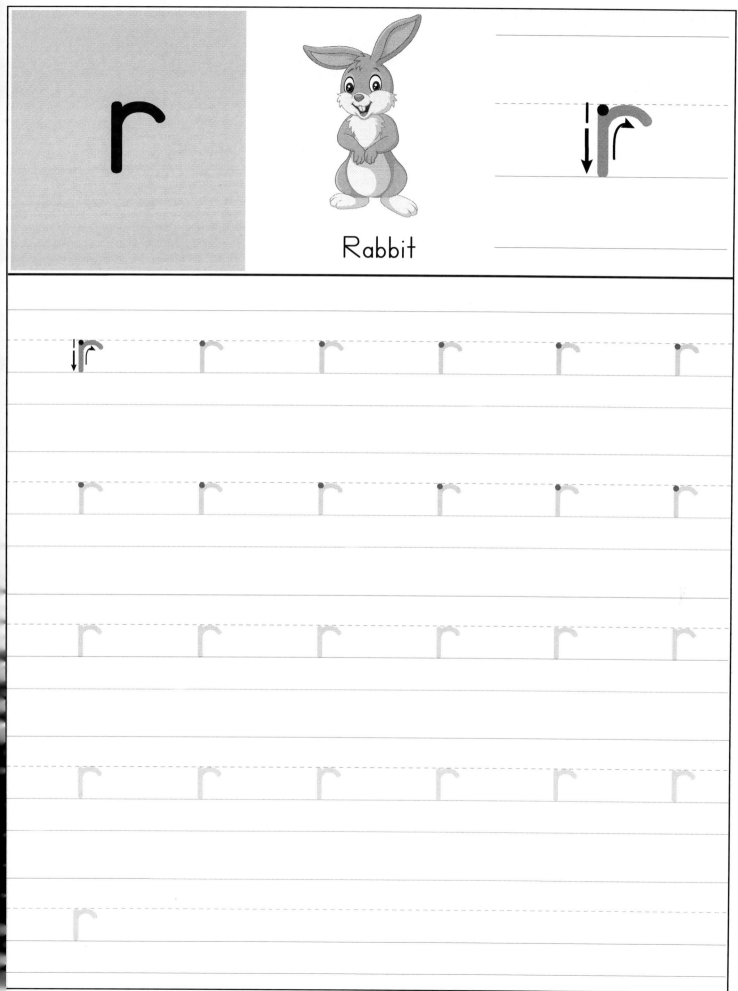

S

Sun

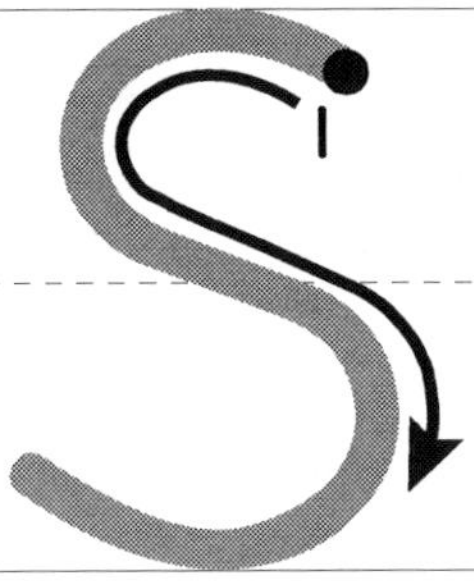

S S S S S S

S S S S S S

S S S S S S

S S S S S S

S

S

Seahorse

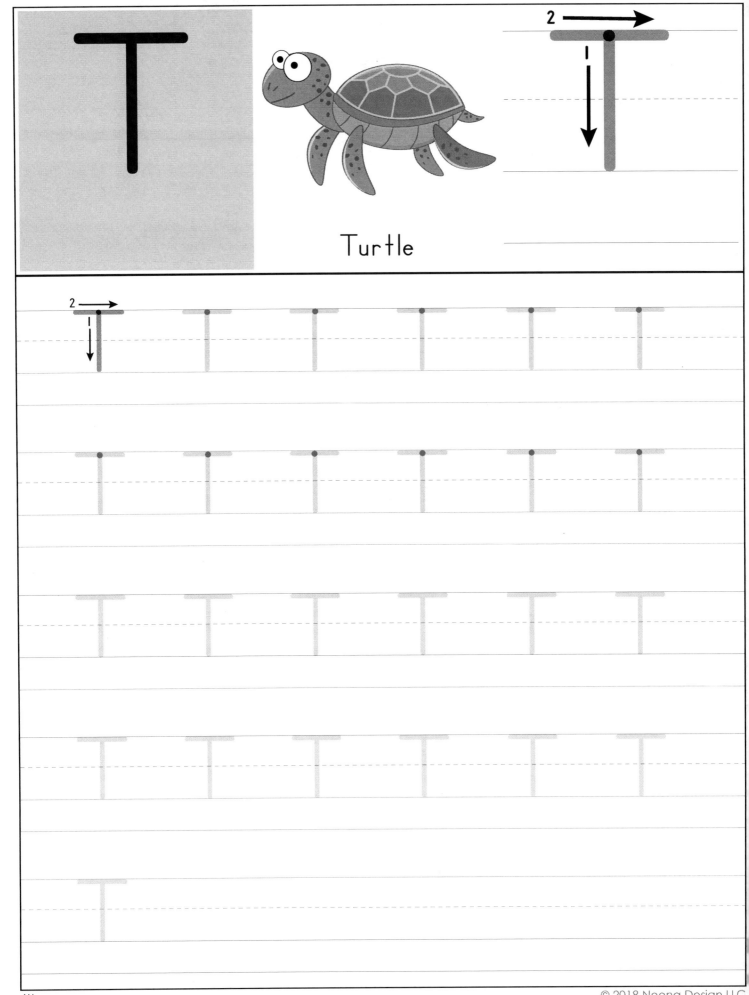

Turtle

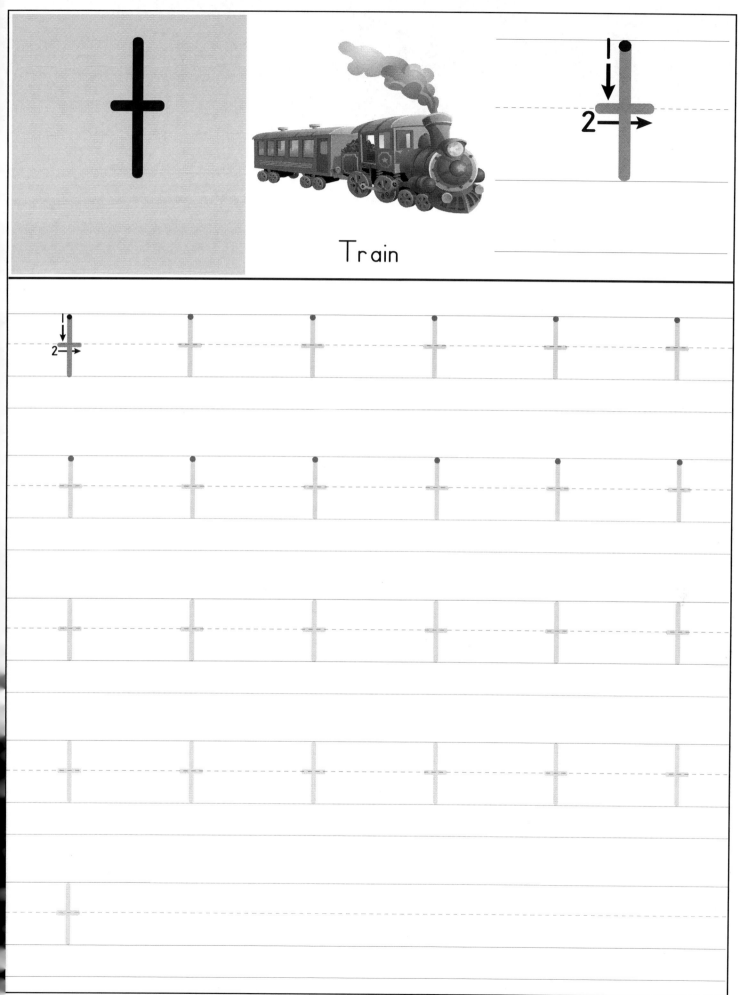

Train

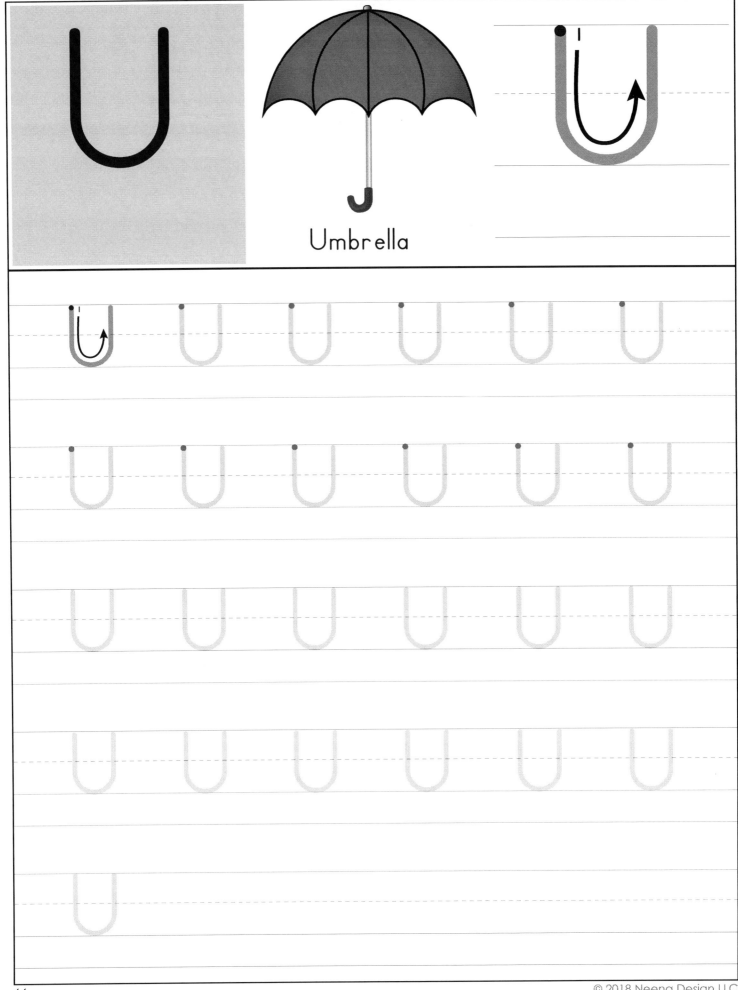

Umbrella

u

Unicorn

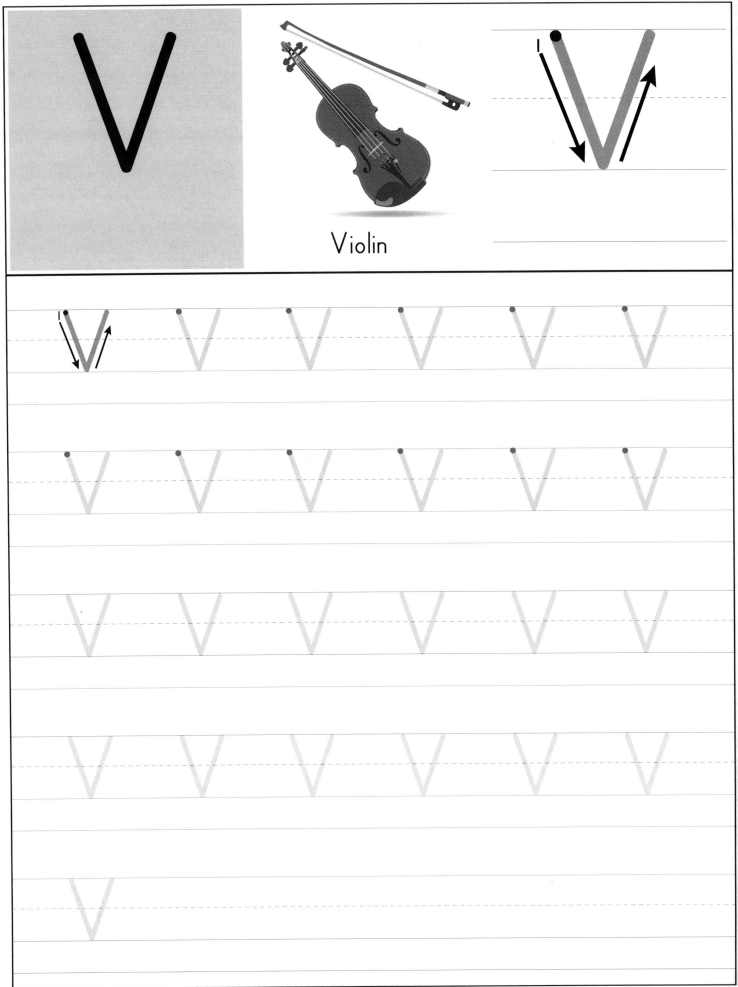

Violin

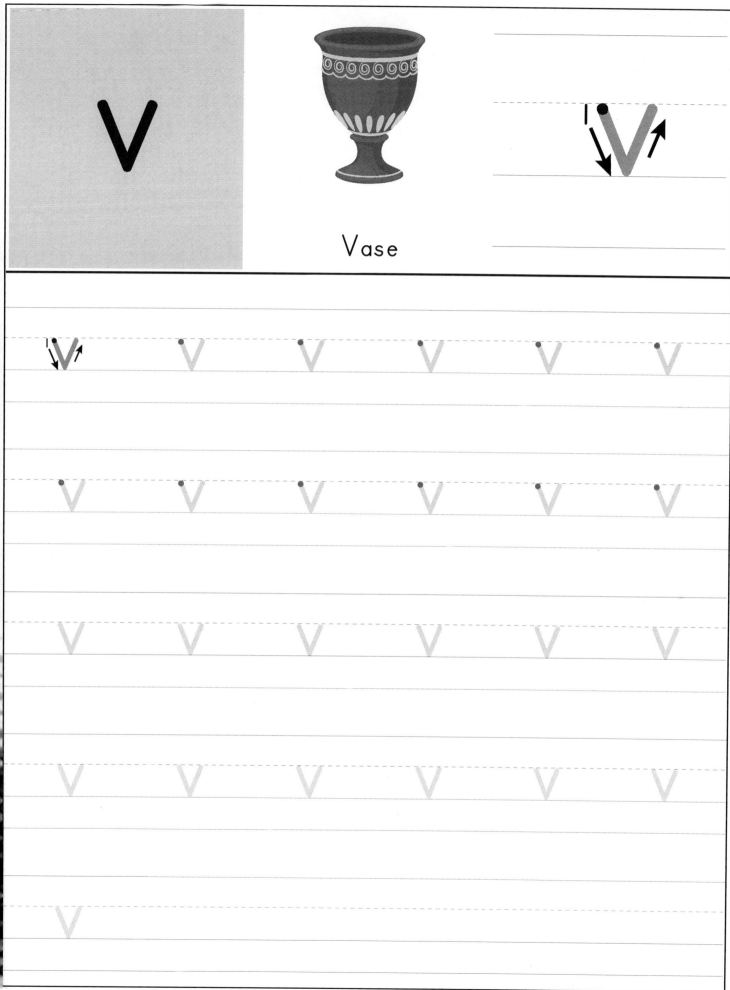

Vase

Watermelon

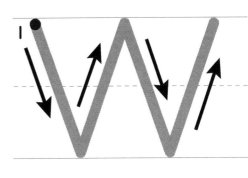

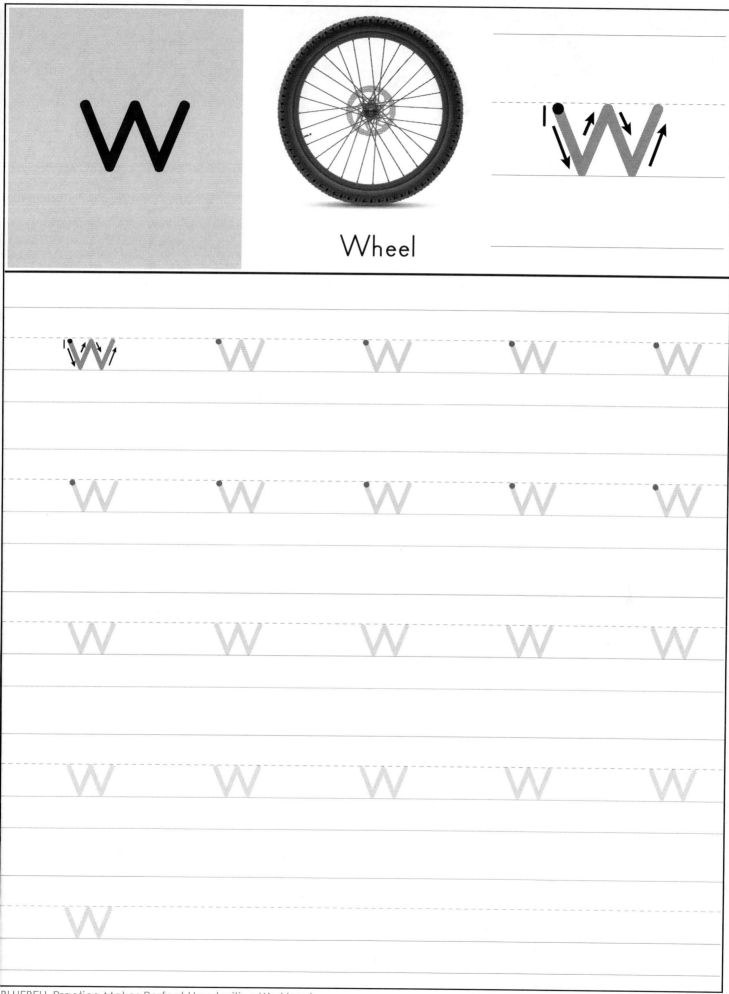

Wheel

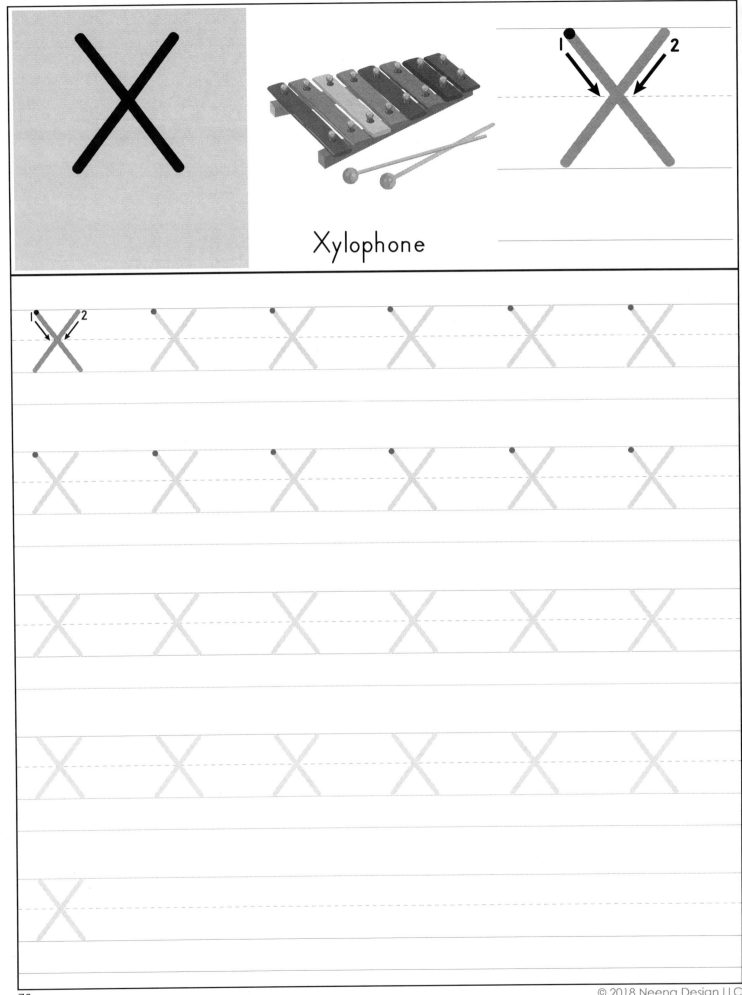

Xylophone

X-ray fish

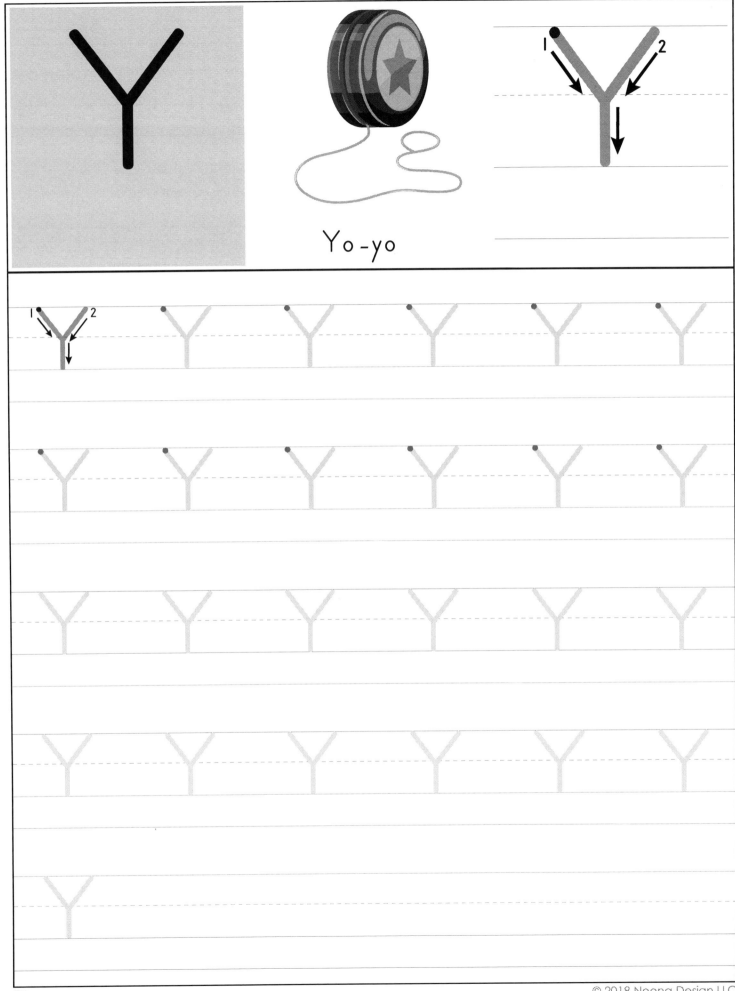

Yo-yo

Yak

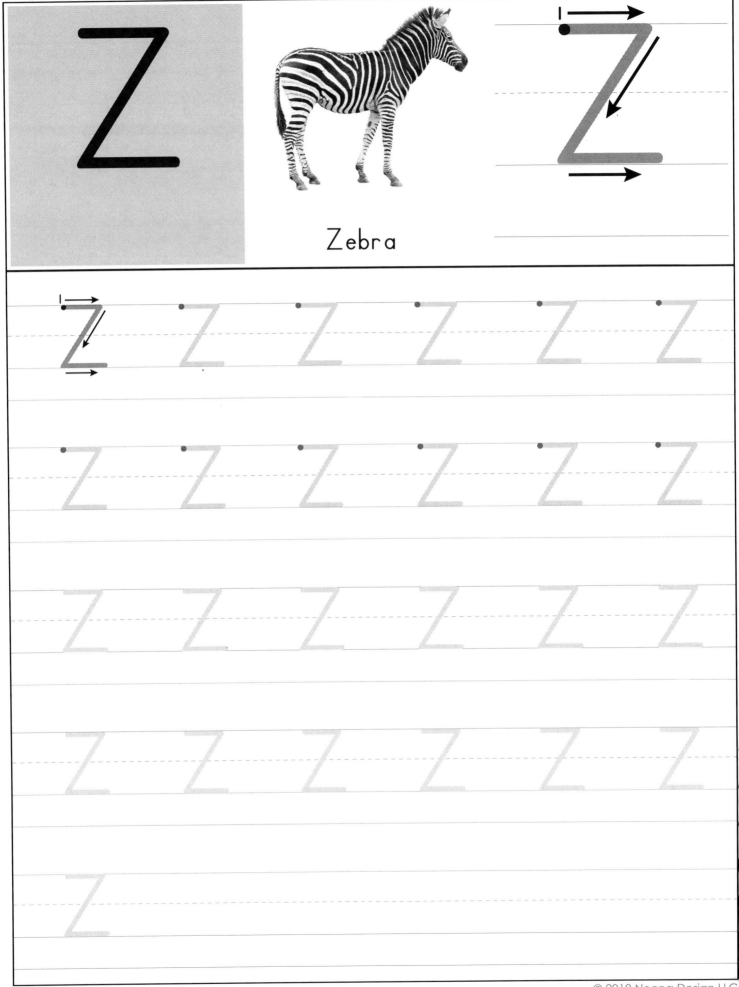

Zebra

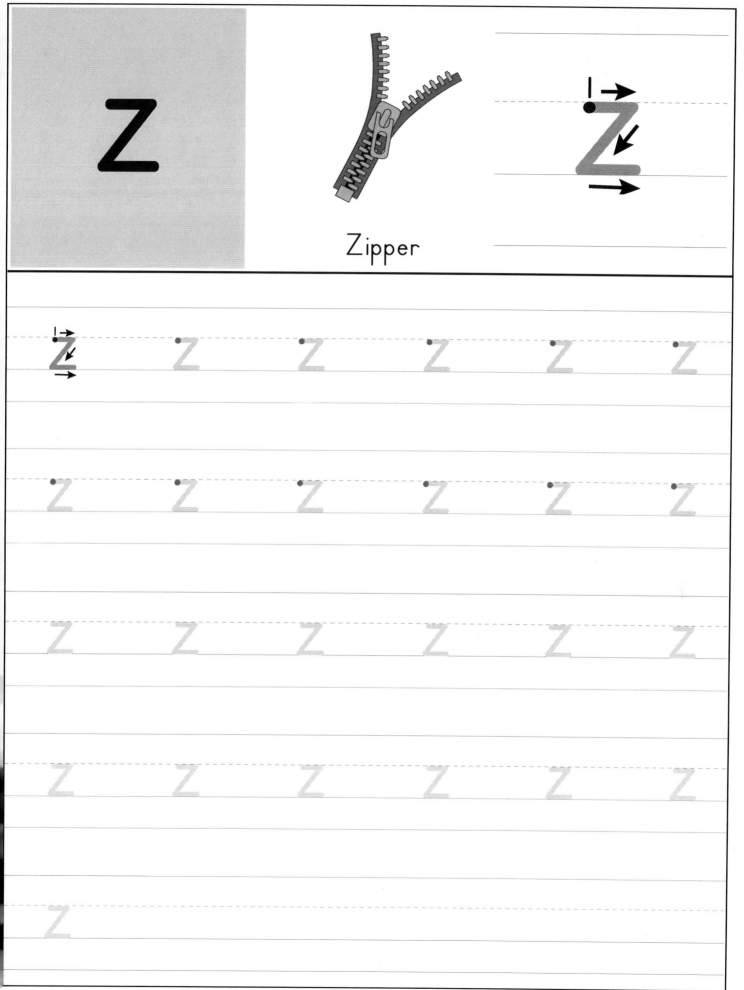

Zipper

Section
3

Review
and
Practice

Review the steps for writing uppercase letters.

Practice writing uppercase letters.

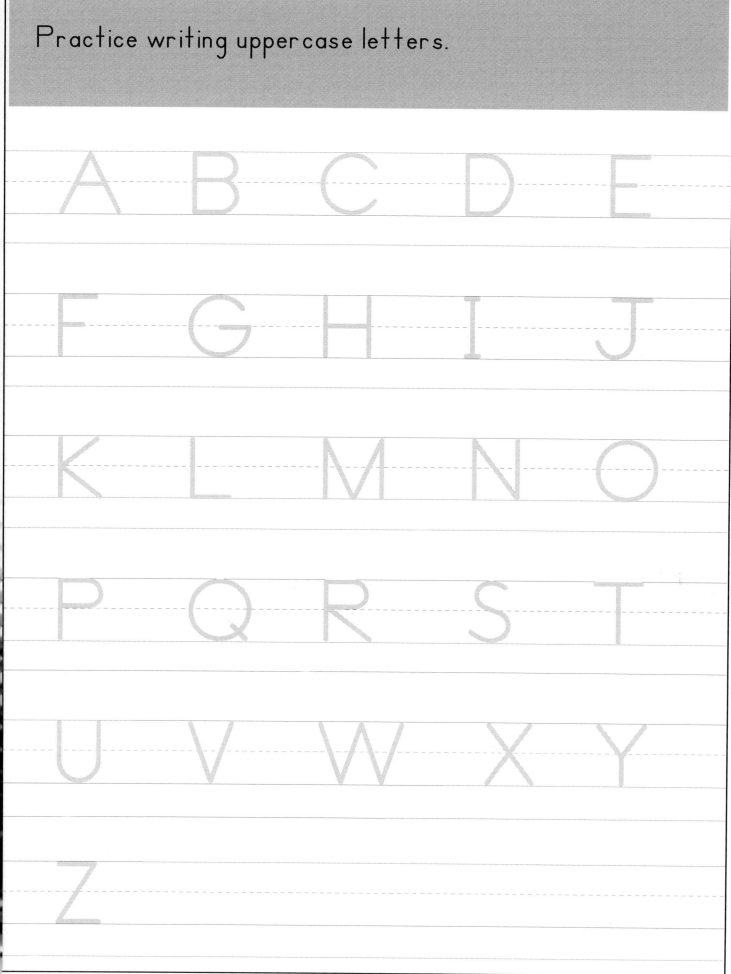

A B C D E
F G H I J
K L M N O
P Q R S T
U V W X Y
Z

a b c d e

f g h i j

k l m n o

p q r s t

u v w x y

z

Practice writing lowercase letters.

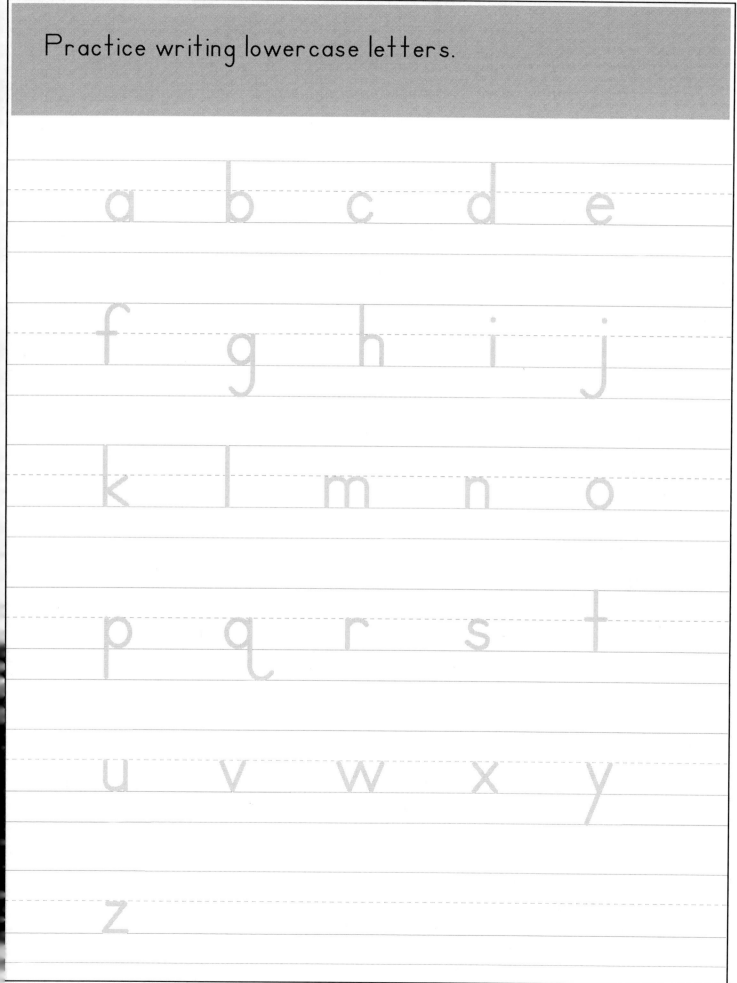

Practice writing uppercase letters.

A

B

C

D

E

F

Practice writing lowercase letters.

a

b

c

d

e

f

Practice writing uppercase letters.

G

H

I

J

K

L

Practice writing lowercase letters.

g

h

i

j

k

l

Practice writing uppercase letters.

M

N

O

P

Q

R

Practice writing lowercase letters.

m

n

o

p

q

r

Practice writing uppercase letters.

S

T

U

V

W

X

Practice writing lowercase letters.

s

t

u

v

w

x

Practice writing uppercase letters.

Y

Z

Practice writing lowercase letters.

y

z

Aa Bb Cc Dd

Ee Ff Gg Hh

Ii Jj Kk Ll

Mm Nn Oo Pp

Qq Rr Ss Tt

Uu Vv Ww Xx

Yy Zz

Section 4

Alphabet
Coloring
Pages

Aa

Apple

Airplane

Abacus

Ant

B b

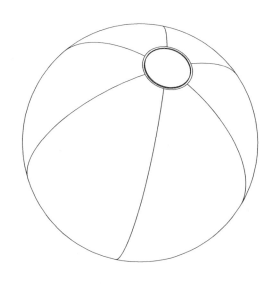

Ball

Butterfly

Bed

Boat

Cc

Castle

Clock

Caterpillar

Car

Dd

Donut

Drum

Dolphin

Donkey

E e

Egg

Eagle

Eggplant

Elephant

F f

Fish

Flower

Flamingo

Fox

Gg

Grapes

Gift

Goat

Giraffe

Hh

Hat

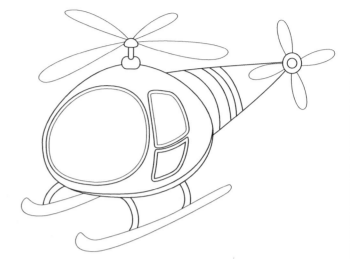

Helicopter

Hen

House

I i

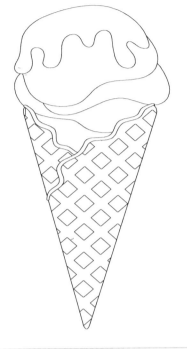

I ce cream

Igloo

Island

Iguana

Jj

Jar

Jelly beans

Jester

Jellyfish

K k

Kitten

Kite

Kangaroo

Kettle

Ll

Ladybug

Lamp

Leaf

Lion

M m

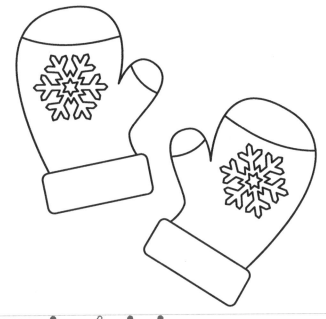

Mittens

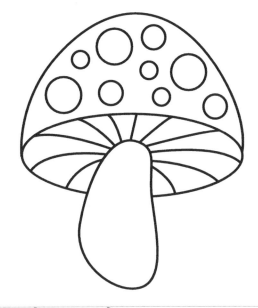

Mushroom

Mouse

Monkey

Nn

Net

Necklace

Nest

Nightingale

Oo

Onion

Owl

Orange

Octopus

P p

Penguin

Parrot

Pumpkin

Peacock

Qq

Queen

Quail

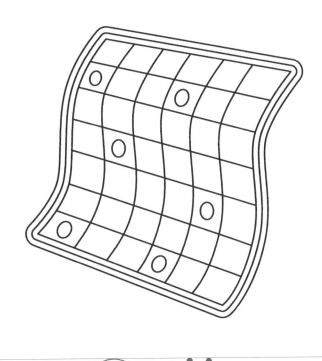

Quilt

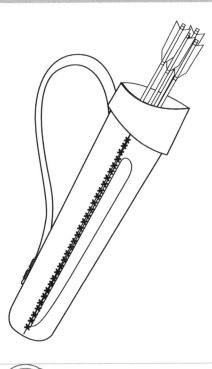

Quiver

Rr

Rabbit

Rainbow

Ring

Rocket

S s

Sun

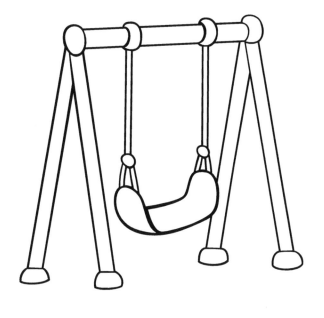

Swing

Squirrel

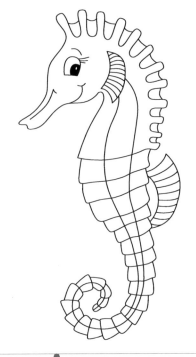

Seahorse

T t

Turtle

Train

Tree

Table

Uu

Unicorn

Umbrella

Unicycle

UFO

V v

Violin

Vase

Van

Vine

W w

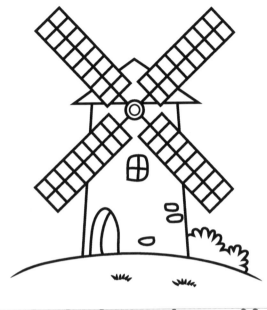

Windmill

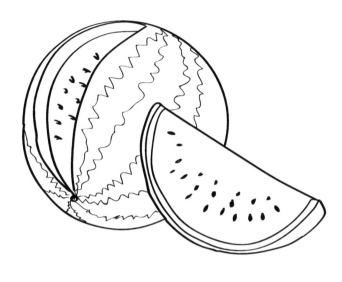

Watermelon

Walrus

Wolf

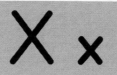

X x

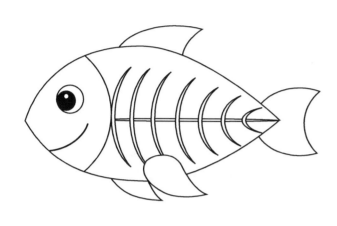

X-ray fish

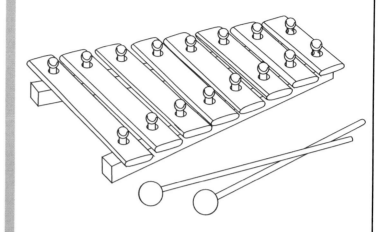

Xylophone

Xanthus

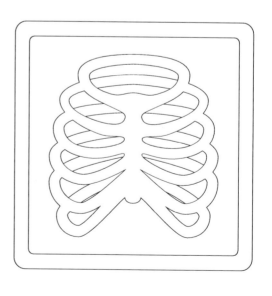

X-ray

Y y

Y o-yo

Y am

Y ak

Y arn

Z z

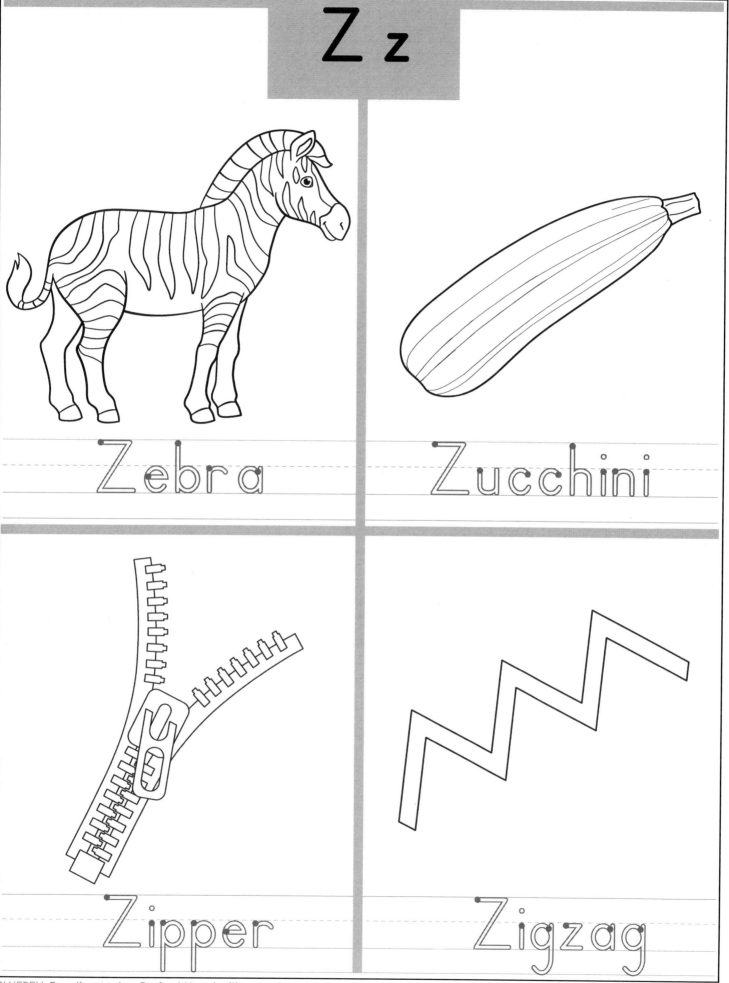

Zebra

Zucchini

Zipper

Zigzag

Made in the USA
Middletown, DE
25 March 2019